Augsburg College
George Sverdrup Library
Minneapolis, Minnesota

INAUGURAL DISSERTATION OF 1770

KANT'S INAUGURAL DISSERTATION OF 1770

TRANSLATED INTO ENGLISH

WITH AN INTRODUCTION AND DISCUSSION

BY

WILLIAM J. ECKOFF

AMS PRESS, INC.
NEW YORK

Reprinted from the edition of 1894, New York
First AMS EDITION published 1970
Manufactured in the United States of America

International Standard Book Number: 0-404-03629-5

Library of Congress Catalog Card Number: 75-124761

AMS PRESS, INC.
NEW YORK, N.Y. 10003

CONTENTS

PART I. INTRODUCTION

		PAGE
1. Summary of Kant's Critical Development	. .	13
2. Kant and Locke	. . . . . .	19
3. Kant and Berkeley	. . . . .	23
4. Kant, Hume and Common Sense	. . .	23
5. The Vital Change	. . . . .	27
6. Leibnitz *versus* Experience	. . . .	28
7. The *Nouveaux Essais* and the *Dissertation*	. .	34
8. Re-Survey in Conclusion	. . . .	37

PART II. TRANSLATION

Dissertation on the Form and Principles of the Sensible and Intelligible World 43

PART III. DISCUSSION: DEVELOPMENTS FROM THE *DISSERTATION*

1. Comments of Lambert and Mendelssohn . 86

(v)

2. The Relation of the *Dissertation* to the Transcendental Dialectic 88
3. The Relation of the *Dissertation* to the Transcendental Æsthetic and Analytic, illustrated from the Amphiboly of Reflective Concepts . . 93
4. A Question and An Answer 97

PREFACE

IN the limits of this paper are set forth: (1) a consideration of the antecedents of the *Dissertation* of 1770 in contemporaneous philosophy, and in Kant's own previous work; (2) an English version of the *Dissertation*; and (3) a comparison of positions occurring in the *Dissertation* with the same as they occur in the Critiques.

No careful observer can doubt that not in Germany only, but in the philosophical university work of the two English-speaking nations also, the cry of "Back to Kant!" is assuming larger proportions. It is the expression of an intelligent perception of the metaphysics demanded by the existing condition and the mutual delimitations of science, of ethics, and of religion, not to speak of the bearing of all these on the grave social facts with which the approaching century is called to deal.

Philosophically, we must get back to firm anchorages. The sociological application of ethics required by the gradual uprising of the fourth estate calls for a complete re-adjustment of ancient land-marks.

Finally, none but the intellectually blind can fail to see the coming of a profound resurgence of religious force. From the dreameries of Aryan Buddhism and its Mahatmas to the practical politics of modern Catholicism and the attendant counter-organization of Protestant fervor, from the tambourines of the Salvation Army to the quiet array of Christian Endeavor and of the King's Daughters, even to the dim realms of spiritism and table-rapping, all is religious ferment.

That modern ethics is deeply influenced by the so-called conflict between religion and science little argument is needed to establish. Beginning from few and lofty intellects, new lights are carried down to the lower ranges of humanity, dimmed, obscured, but only the more disquieting. In spite of science and the old-line ethics, using sometimes as speaking-tubes the ancient creeds, often thrusting them fiercely aside, there is rising again from the deep of human hearts, the cry to the unspeakable depth of the Absolute Fatherhood.

And not less than the speculative, moral, and religious are the practical involutions. The masses are ripening for a social, as toward the end of the eighteenth century they were rising for a political, revolution. It is the part of a fool to deprecate a coming revolution. It is the part of the wise to guide it. After hearing all the metaphysical explanations for the *Terreur* of the French revolution in comparison with Anglo-Saxon overturns, it occurs to one that it is easily explicable. The latter were not in charge of madmen. Locke was the guiding, steadying, controlling spirit over the spirits of the men that controlled the American Revolution, little as the influence of his writings—the circulation of which in the Colonies was comparatively immense—is suspected by one school of writers on American history.

Ideas make facts; Platonic as the expression may sound in some ears, it is true, at all events, of historical facts. Is not the whole program of the nature-hatred and ecstatic monkery of medieval history in a line of Augustine—"*Noli foras ire; in te ipsum redi; in interiore homine habitat veritas ?*"—Is not the French Revolution the carrying-out of the Montesquieu program first, of the Rousseau program later on? At present we need not fear the people, but we do need to fear the sophist. This is the renaissance of the sophists. As in the time of Socrates, the old hold of professed religions is being loosed, narrow patriotism is dissolving into individualism and cosmopolitanism, and a physiological psychology is rampant on ground once reserved to ethics. A sharp and logical questioning of the sophists is imperative.

To-day an individual Socrates is impossible. The disease is world-wide. But the scientist if content modestly to claim all that he can hold, the moralist sincere in his appeal not to what man would but to what he should, the religionist not clamorously affirming a chemical proof for God, Freedom, and Immortality, but deep and strong enough to take it in the imperative of the moral law and to see it foreshadowed in the teleology of nature,—each and every one will find his impregnable Magna Charta in the Critiques of Kant.

And if we must have a revolutionary program, what safer, since of the nature of the Social Contract it must be—what especially safer for us, whose independence as a nation is a vindication of Locke, the Rousseauist before Rousseau—than the sublimated Rousseauism of Kant? A nation substantially free does not reform by fire-brand. Truly as beautifully says Bluntschli: "Rousseau carried the wildly-flaming torch through street and market-place; Kant in a thousand studies lighted the quiet lamps and candles."[1]

We shall, by going back to Kant, lose nothing that is worth keeping of Hegel, of Schelling, of Fichte, or of Kant himself, and we shall get a good deal more than we have ever yet done out of the much-neglected Herbart, on whom we depend after all for the evolution of a philosophy of pedagogy.

But whether we gain or lose by going back to Kant, there

[1] *Geschichte der neueren Statswissenschaft*, S. 373.

PREFACE

is for the present nothing else to do. You cannot get either scientist, or religionist, or theoretical statesmanship, to make much of Fichte or Schelling. We shall be lucky if we stop at Herbart, and are not driven back on a section of Leibnitz. Of Hegel, the world of thought appears to have had for the present about as much as it will stand. The cause assigned by Heine for the pallor of the arch-enemy is about to cease.

> Zwar ist er bleich, doch ist's kein Wunder;
> Sanskrit und Hegel studirt er jetzunder.

It is the conviction of the writer that understanding Kant can be achieved best, not by the utilization of any of the commentaries whose number makes one deplore that editor Omar of the Alexandrian Library is a myth, but by calling on Kant to explain himself. As a part of the plan for collecting the elicited responses, a series of monographs was prepared covering the field of the pre-critical work of Kant in Kant's own language, with no more additions from the writer than would suffice for connective tissue. These monographs, accumulated during studentship in Columbia College, were roughly run together into a text of about three hundred pages.

It is accordingly proposed either to issue the work in the original monographs or as a connected introductory text. The present paper is best judged as a part of this larger plan, disjoined and prepared for separate publication. Kant's language is adhered to only as far as smoothness of presentation permits. References by volume and page to Hartenstein's eight-volume edition (1868) will enable the reader to determine the amount of deviation in each case, as well as to discriminate additions by the writer, which in this isolated paper have necessarily been expanded in order measurably to establish his conception of the subject. Italics are always Kant's own. As far as possible Max

Müller's terminology has been adopted, as being familiar to the English reader. The writer is not without hope that even in this detached form the paper may be of some trifling service in elucidating the Critique, either autodidactically or in preparation for classes.

THE DISSERTATION

De Mundi Sensibilis atque Intelligibilis Forma et Principiis

THE TURNING POINT IN KANT'S PHILOSOPHY

PART I

INTRODUCTION

1. Summary of Kant's Critical Development

LICHTENBERG classified man as an *Ursachenthier*, a cause-seeking animal. This appetite for causes was analyzed by Hume into a habit of association. Disregarding the Associationists and the Scottish school of philosophy, Hume's lasting influence on the history of philosophy arose from his becoming the metaphysical conscience of Kant. The whole development dates back to Locke. Locke's philosophy, to quote Kant, was a noögony or, as he elsewhere puts it, a physiology of the understanding.

In a less Baconian direction, continental Cartesianism emulated mathematics in the effort to arrive at apodictic certainty through deductive dogmatism. Leibnitz, formulated by Wolff, became dominant in Germany. Kant's pre-critical metaphysics is, therefore, substantially Leibnitzian.

Newton caused a methodical change in the youthful metaphysics of Kant. From propounding the Theory of the Heavens, that was wrought out by Laplace, Kant went on into geographical and geological studies, anticipating often modern views. From the dwelling-place of man his reflection was led to anthropology. Then came the era of the Rights of Man. We have Kant's verdict: "Rousseau has set me right."

Uniting these influences with a Christian education "than which none better was imaginable," set Kant the scientist, deeming causality "a mental law which under no circumstances is it permitted to desert, and from which no phenomenon must be excepted," at variance with Kant the moralist, destined to preach to the world the Categorical Imperative of duty, with its implications of freedom and personal responsibility. If phenomena are things in themselves, freedom cannot be saved.[1] But, for moral actions, freedom must be saved. Hence the necessity for Kant of both a Sensible and an Intelligible world.

Without freedom is impossible the entire practical philosophy of Kant. He terms practical whatever is possible through freedom.[2] He needs, therefore, an intelligible, *i. e.* moral, world.[3]

But all our knowledge begins with the senses.[4] In fact, all cognition of which man is capable is sensuous. Our knowledge of objects of sense through connected perceptions is experience.[5] Therefore, in point of time, knowledge does not precede experience.[6] Our theoretical knowledge, including under sense the inner and the external senses, never transcends the field of experience.[7] There is but one experience, just as there is only one space and only one time.[8]

[1] III, 373.   [2] III, 529.   [3] III, 534.
[4] III, 247.   [5] VIII, 535.   [6] III, 33.
[7] VIII, 535.   [8] III, 574.

Only in experience is truth;[1] hence the need of a sensible, uninterfered with by the intelligible world.

If we are to have no such interference, all phenomena must exist in one nature. Without such unity *a priori*, no unity of experience, and therefore no determination of objects in experience, would be possible.[2] Nature, in the empirical sense of the word, means the coherence of phenomena in their existence, according to necessary laws.[3] Experience, and therefore the objects of experience, would be impossible without causal connection.[4] The determining an occurrence in time, that is, the occurrence itself as pertaining to experience, would be impossible did it not fall under such a dynamic rule. By determining by means of the law of causality an object corresponding to a concept, a represented occurrence has objective validity, or, in a word, truth.[5] But in time nothing can determine anything else, except it be the cause of the latter's determinations.[6]

But will not Hume's habitual association do as a definition of cause?—Kant thinks not. The semblance of a conviction, based on subjective association and mistaken for the perception of a natural affinity, cannot balance the misgivings justly roused by such bold proceedings. The proofs, like streams that have broken their banks, run wildly across the fields wherever the inclination of some hidden association may chance to lead them. We must show the possibility of arriving synthetically and *a priori* at a certain knowledge of things not contained in the concept of the thing.[7]

The usual assumption is that our knowledge must conform to the object. On this supposition, any attempt to settle anything concerning an object by *a priori* concepts intended to enlarge our experience suffers shipwreck. Let us try

[1] IV, 122.   [2] III, 191.   [3] III, 191.   [4] III, 518.
[5] III, 521.   [6] III, 189.   [7] III, 518.

whether we shall succeed better on the hypothesis that the objects must conform to our cognition.¹

We thus assume concepts having an *a priori* reference to objects. These concepts are neither empirical intuitions nor pure intuitions. They are acts of pure thought.² The mind of man carries order and regularity into the phenomena which we call nature. If originally it had not placed them there, it would never find them in nature.³ We thus form by anticipation an idea of a science of the knowledge which belongs to the pure understanding and reason, and by which we think objects entirely *a priori*. The science which determines the origin, the extent, and the objective validity of such knowledge may be called *transcendental logic*.⁴

Of the understanding, various definitions have been given. It has been called the spontaneity of knowledge—as opposed to the receptivity of the senses—the faculty of thinking, of concepts, of judgments. These explanations closely examined amount to the same. We may now characterize the understanding as *the faculty of rules*.⁵

Objective rules, necessarily inherent in our knowledge of an object, are called laws. Although experience teaches us many laws, yet these are only particular determinations of higher laws. The highest among them, to which all others are subject, spring *a priori* from the understanding. They are not derived from experience, but, on the contrary, impart to phenomena their regularity, and thus make experience possible. The understanding therefore is not only a power of making rules by a comparison of phenomena. It is itself the law-giver of nature. Without the understanding, nature, that is, a synthetical unity of the manifold of phenomena according to rules, would be nowhere to be found, as phenomena cannot exist without us, but only in our sensibility.⁶

¹ III, 17, 18. ² III, 85. ³ III, 582.
⁴ III, 85. ⁵ III, 583. ⁶ Ibid.

The reply of Kant to Hume, in which the Königsberg philosopher makes causality a "function of the understanding" is of the profoundest significance. The proclamation of the human mind as the law-giver of nature marks a turning-point in the whole history of metaphysics. Kant was the first who dared say: it may sound exaggerated and absurd to say that the understanding is the source both of the laws and of the unity of nature. It is correct nevertheless, and accords with experience.[1] It is like the thought of Copernicus, who, finding the explanation of the heavenly motions proceeded poorly on the assumption of the whole host of stars turning around the spectator, made trial of better success by turning the spectator and leaving the stars at rest.[2]

The thought is of Leibnitzian genealogy. Lockean sensualism subscribed the scholastic *Nihil est in intellectu quod non fuerit in sensu.* It was Leibnitz who added: *Nisi intellectus ipse,*[3] in a sense very different from Cartesian Dualism.

However, Kant puts in as strong an anti-Leibnitzian ingredient. It would vitiate his concepts of sensibility and phenomena and render his doctrine useless and empty if he were to accept the Leibnitz-Wolffian view that our whole sensibility is but a confused representation of things, containing what belongs to them under an accumulation of qualities and partial concepts, which we do not consciously disentangle. The distinction between confused and well-ordered concepts, he objects, is logical only. It does not touch the contents of our knowledge. By thus representing the difference between the sensible and the intelligible as only logical, the Leibnitz-Wolffian philosophy gave a wrong direction to all investigation into the nature and origin of our knowledge. That difference, according to Kant, is in

[1] III, 583.   [2] III, 18.   [3] Nouveaux Essais, II, 12.

truth transcendental. It affects not only the form, as more or less confused, but the origin and contents. By our sensibility we do not know the nature of things confusedly. We do not know it at all. Apart from our subjective condition, the object, as represented and qualified by our sensibility, is nowhere to be found. It cannot possibly be found, since its form, as phenomenal appearance, is determined by those very subjective conditions.[1] This intuition is *a priori* in us. It is in us before any perception of an object.[2]

How can an external intuition preceding the objects take place in the mind, and how can it *a priori* determine the objects? Obviously it can do so only by inhering in the subject as its formal capacity for being affected by objects so as to obtain an immediate presentation or intuition of the same. In other words, it can only do so by being the general form of the external sense of the subject.[3]

Why did Kant place himself in strenuous opposition to Leibnitz at so vital a point? The reply can be put into a single sentence: Our explanation alone renders comprehensible the possibility of geometry considered as a synthetic *a priori* cognition.[4]

An equally good *a priori* basis for number is furnished by Kant's metaphysical treatment of time. The pure image of all quantities for the external sense is space. The pure image of all objects of sense, generally, is time. Now, the pure schema for quantity, regarded as a concept of the understanding, is number. Number is a presentation comprising the successive addition of homogeneous units. Number, therefore, is simply unity in the synthesis of the manifold in a homogeneous intuition accomplished by my generating time itself while apprehending my intuition.[5]

---

[1] III, 73. [2] III, 61. [3] Ibid.
[4] Ibid. [5] III, 144.

Having made time and space forms of human intuition, and the Categories, or pure concepts of the understanding, functions of the "unity of apperception," Kant relegates to the Dialectics of Pure Reason the ideas relating to God, universe and soul. They are regulative, not constitutive. The Critical System is based upon the thesis: The speculative use of reason does not reach beyond the objects of possible experience.[1]

We have outlined the Critical System. The caution is not amiss that this outline lays no claim to completeness. For instance, Kant is responsible for much demolition and refashioning of Aristotelian logic. Outside of the Baconian rebellion, his attempt is the first attended with important and lasting consequences. Our dealings with the Critique are limited by a special purpose. This outline, besides, is merely for preliminary orientation. At this moment we are content to have shown that Kant, trained in natural science and mathematics, primarily under Newton, and dissatisfied with the psychogenetic philosophy of Locke, as well as with the rationalistic metaphysics of Leibnitz, mainly because he understood as none before him the force of Hume's argument, made the attempt to pilot human reason between the two rocks of mysticism and skepticism.[2] He set aside the noumenal or intelligible world to Practical Reason, whilst assigning to speculative reason the definite limits of experience. He wished to keep open to human reason its entire field of activity in the division suited to its purposes.[3]

2. *Kant and Locke*

One principle is of fundamental importance to understanding Kant. The Critique is a treatise on metaphysics. It is not a treatise on psychology. It considers not the origin

[1] IV, 364, note.   [2] III, 113   [3] Ibid.

but the validity of the basic assumptions implied in thinking. All our knowledge begins with the senses.[1] But that the objects themselves, as for instance, material nature, should be subject to principles determined according to mere concepts, is something, at all events, extremely contradictory.[2] It is this seeming impossibility, which is yet a fact, on which Kant establishes his critical principles. The beginning of our knowledge from the senses is a beginning in time and can furnish no starting-point for Kant, though it might for Locke, Kant refusing to acknowledge Locke's "falsely pretended genealogy of metaphysics from the rabble of common experience." Kant does not controvert the psychogenetics of Locke. He simply does not acknowledge them as metaphysics.

Kant's classification of philosophical schools is, on this principle of division, perfectly plain. With reference to the origin of the pure concepts of reason, namely, whether they are derived from experience or originate independently of experience, in reason, Aristotle may be looked upon as the head of the Empiricists, Plato as that of the Noölogists, Locke, who followed Aristotle, and Leibnitz, who followed Plato—though at a sufficient distance from his mystical system—have not been able to bring the dispute to any conclusion.

Epicurus, never allowing his syllogisms to go beyond the limits of experience, was far more consistent in his sensual system, at least, than Aristotle and Locke, more particularly the latter, who, having derived all concepts and principles from experience, goes so far in their application as to maintain that the existence of God and the immortality of the soul, both of which lie beyond possible experience, can be proved with the evidence of a mathematical proposition.[3] By observations on the play of our thoughts and on the

[1] III, 247. [2] III, 249. [3] III, 561.

natural laws of the thinking self derived from them, we have before us an empirical psychology, a psychology of the internal sense, which perhaps explains its manifestations, but can never help us to understand properties that do not fall under experience, or to teach apodictically anything touching the nature of thinking beings in general.[1]

Kant admits that an investigation of the first efforts of our cognitive faculty, beginning with single perceptions and rising to general concepts, is no doubt very useful; we thank Locke for having been the first to open the way.[2] But he complains that Locke by his ultra-experiential extension of experiential results threw wide open the gates to mysticism, since reason, once having authority on its side, is not to be kept within bounds by recommendations of moderation.[3] The "mysticism" hits at Berkeley, for in Kant's belief all genuine Idealism is of mystic intent, and can be of none other.[4] However that may be, the Categories are concepts *a priori*. They are independent of experience.

Does Kant owe nothing to Locke? Through a certain range of their intellects there is much kinship. A contemporary reviewer of the Critique of Pure Reason delivered himself of the opinion: "This work is a system of the higher Idealism." With a sarcastic acerbity unusual in him, Kant replies: "For goodness' sake don't say *higher*. As to high towers and the metaphysically great men resembling them, there is usually about them much wind. They are not for me. My place is the fertile *bathos* of experience."[5] A rejoinder like this might as easily be Locke's as Kant's. Other passages may be quoted having a Lockean cast, such as the illustrative paragraph, which was much condensed in the second edition of the Critique of Pure Reason, at the end of

[1] III, 277. [2] III, 108. [3] III, 113.
[4] IV, 123, note. [5] IV, 121, note.

the treatment of Space.¹ From such passages we might go on to: The *image* is a product of the empirical faculty of the productive imagination, while the *schema* of sensuous concepts, such as of the figures in space, is a product, and, so to speak, a monogram of the pure imagination *a priori*;² and thence to: Even the representation of space and time is a pure schema, always referring to that productive imagination.³ One might thus be tempted to make out a genealogy from Locke for the Form and Principles of the Sensible World.

But we are to take into serious account such passages as the following, written, by the way, against Berkeleian Idealism, not for or against Locke. It was conceded long before Locke's time, generally, however, after him, that without prejudice to the actual existence of external things, we may say of a multitude of their predicates that they do not pertain to these things, but to their phenomena only, having outside of our representation no existence of their own. Here belong warmth, color, taste, etc. Not the slightest ground of inadmissibility can be alleged against my adding to the number of phenomena the so-called primary qualities of bodies, extension, place, and space, with all that appertains to it.⁴

Was Kant's classical division of judgments into analytical and synthetic suggested by Locke?—The following is Kant's reply: I find a suggestion of this division as early as Locke's Essay on the Human Understanding. Having spoken of the different connection of presentations and judgments and its sources, one being placed in identity or contradiction—analytical judgments—the other in the existence of the presentations in one subject—synthetic judgments—he confesses that our knowledge—*a priori*—of that existence is very narrow and almost nothing. There being in what he

[1] III, 63.   [2] III, 143.   [3] III, 151.   [4] IV, 38.

says of this species of cognition so little that is definite and reduced to rules, it is no wonder that no one, especially not even Hume, has taken occasion thence to engage in reflections on this species of propositions. Principles general and yet definite one does not readily learn from others who had but a dim foreshadowing. One must have arrived at them by independent reflection. After that one finds them where certainly one should not at first have done so, because even the authors themselves were not aware that such an idea lay at the core of their remarks. People that never do any independent thinking, nevertheless possess acuteness of sight to detect what is pointed out to them to have been already said in places where previously nobody could see it[1].

3. Kant and Berkeley

Having dealt elsewhere with the alleged kinship between Criticism and Berkeleianism, we shall here dismiss the subject with a single remark: The one reference in the Dissertation to empirical Idealism is against it[2].

4. Kant, Hume and Common Sense

The German homologue of the Common Sense of the Scottish philosophy is the appeal to the gesunden Menschenverstand. Of this common sense and commonplace philosophy, Mendelssohn and Basedow were well-known representatives. Kant's verdict on this school we have, as we have his verdict on Associationism, namely, incidentally to a discussion of Hume. We shall give it substantially in the words of Kant:

Hume in the main started from a single but important metaphysical concept, namely, that of the connection of cause and effect, implying the consequent concepts of force, action, etc. He challenged reason to answer to his question-

[1] IV, 18.   [2] II, 404.

ing that anything can be so qualified that by positing it something else is posited necessarily. He proved that it is wholly impossible for reason to think such a connection *a priori* from concepts. He inferred that in the concept of causality reason is completely self-deceived, certain presentations having been brought by imagination and experience under the Law of Association, and the subjective necessity thence arising having been palmed off for objective. Hence he concluded that reason has no faculty to think such connections, even in a general way. If, nevertheless, it did do so, its concepts would be mere fictions, and its pretended *a priori* cognitions nothing but common experience with a false hall-mark. This was as much as to say: There is no such thing as metaphysics, and there can be none. The conclusion, though hasty and incorrect, was at least founded on investigation.

It is impossible to see without a degree of pain how the point of the problem was completely missed by his opponents, Reid, Oswald, Beattie, and finally Priestley. In order to satisfy the problem, his opponents would have had to penetrate very deeply into the nature of reason, as far as exclusively occupied with pure thought, That did not suit them. Consequently they invented the commodious way of braving it out by an appeal to Common Sense. Common Sense is a great gift of heaven, but to appeal to it as an oracle when insight and science have run down to heel-taps is a subtile invention for enabling the shallowest babbler bravely to engage and hold out with the profoundest mind. The appeal is nothing but an appeal to the judgment of the crowd. I should fancy Hume's claim to common sense was as good as Beattie's, and besides he could claim something that Beattie did not possess, to wit, critical reason.

I frankly confess that David Hume's reminder was exactly what broke my dogmatic slumbers and gave a totally different direction to my investigations in the field of speculative philosophy. Commencing from a well-founded, though not elaborated, thought, one may fairly hope, by continued reflection, to get on farther than the keen-witted man whom one had to thank for the first light. I soon found that the concept of cause and effect is far from being the only one by which the understanding thinks *a priori* the connection of things; but that, on the contrary, these concepts constitute the whole of metaphysics. When from a single principle I had succeeded in ascertaining their number, I went at deducing them, being now assured that they were not, as Hume had doubted, derived from experience, but from the pure understanding.[1]

To perceive the force of this confession as to Hume's influence on Kantian metaphysics it must be remembered that Kant divided all contestants in the field into Naturalists and Scientists. The first class includes the common sense controverters of Hume, described thus: The naturalist of pure reason lays down as his principle that more can be achieved by means of common reason, without science, than through speculation. It is as if one should maintain that the magnitude and distance of the moon can be better determined by the naked eye than by a roundabout mathematical calculation. This is mere misology reduced to principles.[2] It is plain that Kant did not need to be delivered from the Common Sense or Naturalist philosophers by Hume.

Those following a *scientific* method have the choice of proceeding either *skeptically* or dogmatically.[3] In Kantian phraseology, dogmatism, therefore, applies both to the sensualism of Locke and the rationalism of Leibnitz. The awakening and directive power of Hume must be measured upon this understanding of the term.

[1] IV, 6, 7, 8.   [2] III, 562.   [3] Ibid.

What has been said in reference to Locke and Kant is applicable to Kant and Hume. Through a certain range their minds were profoundly similar. The following remarks of Kant on Hume are just as true of himself. Hume called this destructive philosophy itself metaphysics, and attributed to it great value. Metaphysics and morals, he says, are the most important branches of science; mathematics and natural science are not worth half as much. But in this passage the acute man had reference only to the negative use, which results from the moderation of the exaggerated claims of speculative reason in removing the many endless and persecuting quarrels which confuse mankind.[1]

Kant's cardinal objection to Hume is: He lost out of sight the damage arising from depriving reason of the most important outlooks in whose direction alone it can stake out to the will the highest goal of its endeavors.[2] That Hume obtained no influence on the Practical Philosophy of Kant is, therefore, plain. That his influence on the speculative Kantianism was of the greatest moment is just as obvious. How far had the latter influence gone when the Dissertation was written? We shall venture a hypothesis.

The *Dissertation* consists of two unequally developed parts. What is said on the Sensible World is not far from the Transcendental Aesthetic. Kant's long mathematical training and the impact of Hume's skepticism combined.

The rest of the *Dissertation* by comparison with the Critique is immature. The war on spurious concepts in the latter part of the *Dissertation* is in Hume's spirit, but skepticism has not fully done its work. There are, to be sure, other displacements of Leibnitzian notions, evidently due, however, to Newtonian rather than Humean influences. In

---

[1] IV, 6, note.   [2] Ibid.

the process of developing this portion of the Dissertation into the Transcendental Logic, Hume was overturned by the deduction of the Categories. This, together with the schematism of the understanding and the synthesis of the pure productive imagination, replaces the bare spontaneity of the Dissertation. Kant gave over what he could not hold against skepticism to the Dialectics of Pure Reason, reserving nothing but what he needed for Practical purposes. The Intelligible World was thus partly discriminated against as transcendent; partly, though legitimated as transcendental, it was restricted to its immanent use in experience. Thus vanished the Intelligible World with the sole exception of the empty but necessary notion of the Noumenon $= X$. The reaction of this process of systematization in the Intelligible World upon the Sensible World answers for what difference there is between the Transcendental Aesthetic and the corresponding part of the *Dissertation*.

5. *The Vital Change*

The *Dissertation* is the Promethean statue begun. But the Critique is more than the statue finished. The vital spark has been introduced.

The idea of the Categories of the understanding as functions of the spontaneous "unity of apperception" expanded. Extending upward, the unity of apperception became the supreme regulative where it could no longer be the constitutive principle. Extending through schematism and productive imagination, it fused and welded Transcendental Aesthetic into one system with the other portions of the Critique. This synthesis of the spontaneous unity of apperception is the pervading motor force of the Critique. It is literally the vital principle. It makes the Critique what it is, and what the *Dissertation* is not. Being an all-pervading principle, no one quotation can show its force. The following citations are merely illustrative. Space, represented as an object, as we actually need to do in geometry, contains more than the mere form of intuition, namely, a synthesis of the manifold. In the Aesthetic I enumerated it merely under sensibility, though it presupposes a synthesis not pertaining to the senses.[1] The synthesis of apprehension which is empirical must necessarily conform to the synthesis of apperception which is intellectual and contained wholly *a priori* in the Category. It is one and the same spontaneity, which in the former under the name of imagination, and in the latter under the name of understanding, introduces connection into the manifold intuition,[2] and it is not more strange that the laws of natural phenomena must necessarily agree with the understanding and its *a priori* form, that is, its faculty of generally connecting the manifold, than that the sensuous phenomena themselves must agree with the *a priori* form of sensuous intuition. Phenomena do not exist in themselves, but only relatively to the subject as far as it has senses. Exactly so laws do not exist in the phenomena, but only relatively to the subject in whom these inhere.[3]

This synthesis constituting a single experience, one nature, one sole unity of apperception, is absent from the Dissertation. This vindication of the laws of nature by unity of apperception is far more than a reply to Hume, though a reply to Hume none the less. It marks the introduction of a principle foreign to all previous philosophy. This novel idea of a synthesis by the spontaneous unity of apperception sets the absolute limits to Hume's influence. In the *Dissertation* the skeptical influence was barely begun.

6. *Leibnitz versus Experience*

The highest problem of Transcendental Philosophy is:

[1] III, 132, note.   [2] III, 133, note.   [3] III, 133–4.

How is experience possible?—Space and time subjectively considered are forms of sensibility. But to form a concept of them as objects of pure intuition—without doing which we could say nothing of them—requires *a priori* the concept of a compound. This requires the concept of a synthesis of the manifold. It consequently requires the synthetic unity of apperception in connecting this manifold. But this unity of consciousness by reason of the difference of intuitive presentations of objects in space and time needs different functions in order to connect them. These functions are termed Categories, and are *a priori* concepts of the understanding. They do not of themselves alone form the foundation for the general knowledge of an object, but they do for the cognition of an object given in empirical intuition. This cognition when obtained is experience. The empirical, that by which an object is given as existing, is termed sensation or impression, constituting the matter of experience; called, when connected with consciousness, perception. To this must be added the form, that is to say, the synthetic unity of apperception in the understanding, in order to produce experience as empirical knowledge.[1]

The Leibnitz-Wolffian philosophy was elaborated in the belief that in addition to the Aristotelian law of Contradiction it had given philosophers a new test, the Law of Sufficient Cause, for the existence of things as distinct from their conceptual possibility, and the proposition of the difference between confused and distinct presentation as a discriminative test of intuition from conceptual knowledge.

With all this elaboration, it unwittingly remained in the field of logic. It took not one step forward towards metaphysics, let alone in metaphysics. The proposition: Everything is a consequence, can belong, as far as it goes, to logic

[1] VIII, 536–7.

only. Were it to be valid of things, we should have to regard everything as consequent upon the existence of something else; the Sufficient Cause could be found nowhere. From this absurdity refuge was taken in the proposition that a thing may have the cause of its existence in itself; that it may exist as a consequence of itself. But if the absurdity is not to be obvious, this proposition again must be applied not to things, but only to judgments, and to none but analytical judgments at that.[1]

As to distinct and indistinct presentations, Leibnitz held that the former mode, which Kant calls intuition merely, is really a confused concept of the object. According to Leibnitz, consequently, intuition is distinct from the concepts of things, not specifically, but only in the degree of consciousness. The intuition of a body would give in the continuous consciousness of all the presentations contained in it, a concept of the body as an aggregate of monads. In this way the proposition: Bodies consist of monads, could arise from experience merely by the analysis of the perception, provided we could see sharply enough with an adequate consciousness of the partial presentations[2].

This Leibnitzian view, Kant maintains, is not only subversive of the apodictic certainty of mathematics but opposed to geometrical experience. The co-existence of these monads is represented as possible in space only. The metaphysician of the Leibnitzian school must admit that space is merely the empirical and confused presentation of the co-existence of the manifold externally to each other. If he does, how can he assert the three dimensions of space as an apodictic *a priori* proposition? From the clearest consciousness of all the partial presentations of a body he could not get by analysis the necessity of that proposition. If he assumes it as the necessary *a priori* foundation for every

[1] VIII, 533-40.   [2] Ibid.

bodily presentation, how will he explain the necessity, since this mode of presentation has only empirical origin, which can furnish no necessity? Passing by this requirement, let him assume space with this property of it. No matter what the quality of that alleged confused presentation, geometry demonstrates to him, not by concepts hovering in the air, but by construction of concepts, that space, and hence that which fills it, to wit, a body, absolutely does not consist of monads, that is, simple parts. Thus the confession is forced that intuition, the presentation of space, for instance, on the one hand, and conception, on the other, are modes of presentation of different species. Intuition cannot by merely resolving the confusion of presentation be converted into concepts. Exactly the same reasoning holds for the presentation of time.[1]

The untenableness of the Leibnitzian view becomes more glaring when from mathematics we go on to physics. According to mere concepts of the understanding it is self-contradictory to think of two things as existing outside of each other which in respect to all internal determinations of quantity and quality are absolutely one and the same. It is one and the same thing thought twice. In other words, we have numerically one. This is Leibnitz's Identity of the Indiscernible.

He attached no little importance to it. Nevertheless it runs sharply counter to reason. For it is inconceivable why a drop of water in one place should prevent the existence of an exactly similar drop in some other place. This proves immediately that things in space must not be represented by concepts of the understanding as things in themselves, but according to their sensual intuition as phenomena; that space is not a quality or relation of things in themselves, and that pure concepts of the understanding by themselves constitute no cognition.[2]

[1] VIII, 533–540.   [2] VIII, 542.

The trouble throughout is, we see, that Leibnitz did not recognize *a priori* intuition as a principle at all. He intellectualized it by converting it into confused concepts. This absence of an intuitional principle was the reason why he held to be impossible what could not be represented by pure concepts of the understanding. His principle of Sufficient Cause, *a priori* intuition being dispensed with, and the representation of the principle being thus reduced to mere *a priori* concepts, produced the consequence that all things considered metaphysically are reality and negation, being and non-being. According to him, pain would have for its reason only an absence of pleasure, vice absence of virtuous impulses, and the rest of a body only the absence of moving force. He failed to consider that in intuition, in space, for instance, one reality, namely, a motor force, may be opposed to another reality, namely, a motor force in the contrary direction, while quite analogously, in internal intuition, real motives may be opposed in the same subject. Thus Leibnitz originated the principle, obnoxious to sound sense and even to morality, that all evil considered as cause is equal to zero. His Sufficient Cause, being posited in mere concepts, did not render the slightest assistance in going beyond analytical judgments.

His system of Pre-Established Harmony, though really intended to explain the communion between the soul and the body, had to be directed, to begin with, to the general explanation of the communion of substances, by virtue of which they constitute one whole. Substances, by the very concept, must be represented as completely isolated. If they are to be mundane substances, their community must be purely ideal, and cannot be real physical influence. The originator of their existence must be assumed an artist who has arranged these completely isolated substances so as to harmonize as if they did influence each other. Thus originated the system of Pre-Established Harmony, the oddest figment in philosophy, simply because everything was to be explained by concepts.

Taking, on the contrary, the pure intuition of space as the *a priori* foundation of all external relations, all substances are connected so as to render physical influence possible. They constitute one whole. All things in space forming the world, and there being but one space, several worlds external to each other become impossible. This proposition of the unity of the world is absolutely indemonstrable if the proof is to be by concepts not founded upon intuition.[1]

We have expressly excluded the discussion of Berkeleianism from this paper. But we make an exception of the following quotation, as it is just as applicable to Leibnitzianism: "The thesis of all genuine Idealists, from the Eleatic School down to Bishop Berkeley, is contained in this formula: All cognition by sense and experience is mere seeming; only in the ideas of the pure understanding and reason is truth. The principle perennially ruling and determining my Idealism is, on the contrary: All cognition of things from pure understanding or from pure reason exclusively is mere seeming, and only in experience is truth."[2]

Assigning any concept either to sensibility or to the pure understanding, and calling the assignment its *transcendental place*,[3] the achievement of the Dissertation can be expressed substantially in one sentence. It transfers a series of Leibnitzian concepts from their transcendental place in the pure understanding to their transcendental place in pure intuition. This is the foundation of the Transcendental Aesthetic.

[1] VIII, 544, 545.   [2] IV, 122.   [3] III, 229, 230.

8. *The Nouveaux Essais and the Dissertation*

Of course this is to concede that the building-stones of the Dissertation are by original extraction from the Leibnitzian quarry. One may demur to locating the exact spot whence.

A recent worthy writer fixes upon the *Nouveaux Essais sur l'Entendement Humain*. Having outgrown the metaphysics of the schools, Kant had long examined the theories of the empiricists. They had not satisfied him. On the contrary, his intent remained to find a new foundation for metaphysics, and he followed Lambert's attempt to begin by discriminating the form from the content of cognition. Now, the eternal truths were shown by Leibnitz to be virtually contained in sensuous experience itself as involuntary forms of relation, the reflection of the understanding setting them forth into clear and distinct consciousness. This principle of virtual innateness is the backbone of the Kantian Inaugural Dissertation. The metaphysical truths lie in the soul as laws of its activity, becoming functions on the occasion of experience, and thus the object and the content of cognition by the understanding.[1]

The accent on "virtual innateness" is disputable. In his letter of the 2d of September, 1770, sending the *Dissertation* to Lambert, Kant tells his correspondent: "About a year since I attained that concept which I do not fear ever to be obliged to alter, though I may have to widen it, and by which all sorts of metaphysical questions can be tested in accordance with entirely safe and easy criteria, and a sure decision reached as to whether they are solvable or insoluble. It seems that metaphysics ought to be preceded by an especial, though purely negative, science determining the validity and limits of the principles of sensibility, in order that they may not confuse the judgments concerning objects of pure reason.

[1] Windelband, Geschichte der Philosophie, Freiburg, 1892, s. 367.

Space and time, and the axioms for considering all things under their relations, are, in respect to empirical cognitions, and all objects of the senses, real enough, and actually contain the conditions of all phenomena and empirical judgments. But when something is thought of not at all as an object of the senses, but by a general and pure concept of the reason as a thing or substance generally, very false positions result by subjecting these things to the fundamental concepts of sensibility. Such a propaedeutical discipline would preserve metaphysics proper from all such admixture of the sensuous."

This last, it is submitted, is the only concept set forth in the letter which Kant did not alter but which in the Critique he did expand. This epistolary utterance is a reinsistence on the following passage from the *Dissertation*: "The whole of metaphysical method as regards the sensible and the intellectual amounts in substance to the following precept: Beware lest the principles of sensuous knowledge transgress their proper boundaries and affect the intellectual concepts[1]. The observation that the application of this criterion to the discrimination of principles is both easy and fertile, is amply borne out in the Critique. In the correspondence on the Dissertation between Kant and Lambert as well as between Mendelssohn and Kant, the discussion turns on space and time. Virtual innateness is not considered. Is it possible that Kant and his correspondents both missed completely *den Nerv der Inauguraldissertation*?

An argument which is not mentioned in the place cited from Windelband might be alleged in favor of the *Nouveaux Essais* as the source of the *Dissertation*. Besides being the ripest development of Leibnitz's intellectual philosophy, the *Nouveaux Essais* are a running commentary on Locke's *Essay Concerning Human Understanding*. At that period of

[1] II, 418.

his development, such a simultaneous and adversative elucidation of sensualistic and rationalistic dogmatism must have been to Kant more impressive than probably any other book.

The real difficulty one has in subscribing unconditionally to Windelband's assertion of specific origin is of a general nature. When all is said, the *Nouveaux Essais*, virtual innateness and all, is but the final development of the Leibnitzian Monadology. Now, the fact is, Kant could do a good deal of developing for himself. He was thoroughly versed in Leibnitzianism. On occasion he could write such a Nouveaux-Essaistic passage as this: " No doubt the infinite though extremely obscure perception of the whole universe ever internally present to the soul already contains whatever reality is to be in the thoughts later to be suffused with greater light. The mind from day to day acquires larger cognition merely by turning the attention to some things, while withdrawing from others an equal degree, thus shedding an intenser light upon the former. It certainly does not enlarge the compass of absolute reality, the material of all ideas derived from its nexus with the universe remaining the same. But what is formal, consisting in the combination of notions and the application of the attention to their difference and agreement, is certainly changed in a variety of ways. We make a similar observation on the inherent force of bodies. For motions rightly considered being not realities but phenomena, and the inherent force modified by the impact of an external body resisting intrusion by its inner principle of efficacy with as much power as it acquires in the direction of the impelling body, the sum of reality in the phenomenon of a motion of forces is equivalent to that which from the first inhered in the quiescent body, although the internal force which when at rest is indeterminate as to direction does not acquire direction except by an external impulse."[1]

[1] I, 390–391.

Nor is this comparison; it is argument. Kant has been discussing the proposition: The quantity of absolute reality in the world is naturally not changed, neither increasing nor diminishing,[1] and the parallel we have quoted leads on to the assertion that though the powers of spirits and their progression to higher perfections seem to be exempt from this law, they are bound by the same.[2] It is worth noting that all this appeared in the *Nova Dilucidatio* a decade before the *Nouveaux Essais*. The transmutation of Leibnitzianism by the spatial and temporal requirements of the natural sciences (and these sciences include psychology, cf. IV, 357) is precisely similar to the substitution of real for logical opposition under Sufficient Cause.

This is but one illustration of the continual evolution of Kantian from Leibnitzian ideas under the influence of mathematical and nature studies. One is a little dubious, therefore, whether the universality of the phenomenon is quite sufficiently recognized by Windelband's attempt to narrow down the origin of the *Dissertation* to one work of Leibnitz.

8. Re-Survey in Conclusion

It is difficult for a man who has done good work in a branch other than that in which his greatest successes have lain to obtain all the recognition due to his semi-professional achievement. We speak of Daltonism, though it was Goethe and not Dalton who first discovered color-blindness. Similarly, Kant's Natural History and Theory of the Heavens is dropped out of sight, and the doctrine presented by him is connected with the name of Laplace, from the point of view of the astronomer justly so. When, however, it is remembered that Kant introduced himself to literature by Thoughts on the Correct Estimation of Living Forces, and that prior to the Dissertation he had written papers, short but preg-

[1] I, 339.   [2] I, 390.

nant with sound scientific suggestions on several geological and meteorological subjects, besides lecturing regularly on geography and anthropology, one realizes that his astronomical performance, a significant scientific work, is merely the most salient point of an activity in natural science in accord with the most advanced thoughts of his day, and what is still better, vivified by original reflection and the genuinely scientific spirit. If much of it is obsolete, as the theory of imponderables in *De Igne*, much survives, and all of it bespeaks a man kept aware by the tenor of his daily work that " in experience alone is truth."

But his scientific status is discipleship to Newton. Space, as the presupposition to the existence of bodies, is to him axiomatic; within space and time the existence of motions, the exponents of forces, is a self-evidencing postulate.

He clearly conceived the idea of applying this fertile quantitative realism to psychological subjects.[1] Thence to metaphysics was a short step. The robust Baconian habits of thought which he had acquired had played havoc with the scholastic Aristotelianism, and swept away the False Subtilty of the Four Syllogistic Figures. If he still believed himself able to point out the Only Possible Evidence towards the Demonstration of the Existence of God, the whole method of his argument pointed forward already toward the Critique of Teleological Judgment. He already realized that none but the alleged proof was possible.[2] The alleged proof was in all but form the Ontological Proof. Neither man's existence, nor that of other spirits, nor that of the bodily world, is presupposed. The proof is indeed deduced from the inherent quality of absolute necessity.[3] In order to attain his position on this subject in the Critiques of Pure and

[1] Cf., *The Essay to Introduce the Concept of Negative Quantities into Philosophy.*
[2] II, 198. [3] II, 134.

Practical Reason, it was only necessary for him to convince himself that time and labor are lost on the famous ontological proof.[1] That point once attained, he could calmly say: "It may be allowable to admit the existence of a Being entirely sufficient to serve as the cause of all possible effects, simply in order to assist reason in her search for the unity of causes. But to go so far as to say that *such a being exists necessarily*, is no longer the modest language of an admissible hypothesis, but the bold assurance of apodictic certainty."[2]

He had passed the period when he indulged in Observations on Optimism. His Considerations on the Feelings of the Beautiful and Sublime, for a long time a favorite production with him, shows the germinal connection in his mind between moral and aesthetic beauty, transmitted possibly from Shaftesbury. His Essay on Diseases of the Head was the forerunner of the Dreams of a Ghost-Seer Elucidated by Dreams of Metaphysics; and in its turn the third chapter of the first part of the latter bears a heading which might well be a sub-title to the Critique of Pure Reason: Antikabbala; A Fragment of Common Philosophy for Abolishing Community with the Spirit World.

Let us indicate somewhat more in detail the thread in this twisted strand of development more particularly connected with the *Dissertation*. As early as the *Nova Dilucidatio*, Kant, setting forth only the sinews and joints of the argument, deemed it his business to dissent from the opinions of illustrious men. He insisted on the difference between ratio veritatis and ratio existentiae,[3] on the absurdity of anything having the cause of its existence in itself, contentions which show his lines of approach to the empirical realism of the Critical System. The Leibnitzian affirmation that in the

[1] III, 411.   [2] III, 417.   [3] I, 373.

whole universe no one thing is equal to any other thing, is classified even at this early stage under Spurious Corollaries from the Principle of the Determining Cause—for Kant already refuses the term Sufficient Cause—as of illegitimate derivation.[1]

The Communion of Substances (*Wechselwirkung*) of the Critique, it is worth distinctly emphasizing, because its insertion among the Categories has been held due to a love of symmetry which in a work like the Critique would be simply childish, is fully formulated even here, a quarter of a century before the appearance of the Critique, as a principle, thus: "No change can happen to substances, except as connected with others, their reciprocal dependence determining the mutual alteration of state.[2]" The very first application (usus) of this alleged superfluous principle is directed against the Idealists, the second completely subverts Leibnitz's Pre-Established Harmony by its own internal impossibility, Kant laying claim to being the first to demonstrate that the co-existence of the substances of the universe does not suffice to establish their *nexus*.[3]

The historical origin of the *Wechselwirkung* as a Category apart from causality is plain from the following utterance: It is probable that gravitation is caused by the same nexus of the substances by which they determine space and that it is for this reason the most primitive law of nature, as is the opinion of professed Newtonians. Among those qui se Newtoni asseclas profitentur,[4] Kant, of course, comprises himself.

In his *Monadologia Physica* Kant strove to point to the employment in natural philosophy of metaphysics combined

[1] I, 391. [2] I, 393. [3] I, 396. [4] I 393.

with geometry. He is clear on the inadequacy of sense-perception to furnish metaphysical knowledge. Those in pursuit of the phenomena of nature only are forever as far from a recondite knowledge of first causes as he who by climbing higher and higher toward a mountain-top should persuade himself that he will at last hold the heavens in the hollow palm of his hand.[1]

The Leibnitzian Monadology, a species of enchanted world, an assumption to which the celebrated man was seduced by taking sense-presentations considered as phenomena, not as one should for a species of presentation entirely distinct from concepts, to wit, for intuition. but for a merely confused cognition by concepts,[2] is now completely disestablished in Kant's mind. Its place we find taken by the physical monad. A physical element or monad not only is in space, but fills space.[3] The monad defines the space of its presence by the sphere of the activity by which it restrains the closer approach of the monads which are in turn present to it externally.[4] The force by which a simple physical element occupies its space is the mutually applied force of impenetrability in several elements.[5] But by the force of impenetrability alone bodies would not have definite volume. There is needed the equally inherent force of attraction. Both together define the limit of extension.[6]

Descartes, the founder of modern metaphysics, was, by type of mind, mathematical. Leibnitz, the inventor of the Differential Calculus, was not less eminent as a mathematician than as a metaphysician. By Spinoza the mathematical form in metaphysical disquisition was carried to the last extreme. After such antecedents, the Wolfian school might be excused for believing that the mathematical mode of procedure was the best expository method in philosophy.

[1] I, 459.   [2] VIII, 546–7.   [3] I, 464.
[4] I, 465.   [5] I, 467.   [6] I, 468.

But Kant introduced his *Inquiry into the Evidentness of the Principles of Natural Theology and Morals* by claiming that the question is such that, if properly solved, the solution will give a definite form to higher philosophy. If the method can be established by which the highest possible certainty in this kind of cognition can be attained, and a thorough insight is had into the nature of this knowledge, the everlasting inconstancy of opinions and scholastic sects will be replaced by a method of teaching prescribed invariably, uniting thoughtful minds to consonant endeavors, as Newton's method in natural science changed the laxity of physical hypotheses into a safe procedure in accordance with experience and geometry.[1]

He proceeded to clear the road to the Critique by showing that the entire method of philosophizing was wrong; that the imitation of methematics was futile. For mathematics obtains all its definitions synthetically, philosophy analytically;[2] mathematics considers the universal under the signs in the concrete, philosophy through the signs in the abstract.[3] Hence philosophical certainty is of an altogether different nature from mathematics.[4]

Continuing in this path he published only two years before the *Dissertation* a paper *On the First Ground of the Difference of Regions in Space*. Here the transcendental nature of space is reached at last. The argument containing the illustration of the right and left hands, and of the spherical triangles from opposite hemispheres, is taken over from this essay into the *Dissertation* bodily.[5]

If the exposition has been lucid, we are probably prepared to appreciate the *Dissertation* as a product of evolution.

[1] II, 283.   [2] II, 284.   [3] II, 286.
[4] II, 298.   [5] II, 409.

PART II

De Mundi Sensibilis atque Intelligibilis Forma et Principiis

DISSERTATION ON THE FORM AND PRINCIPLES OF THE SENSIBLE AND THE INTELLIGIBLE WORLD

SECTION I

ON THE IDEA OF A WORLD IN GENERAL

Paragraph 1

As the analysis of a substantial composite terminates only in a part which is not a whole, that is, in a *simple part*, so synthesis terminates only in a whole which is not a part, that is, the *world*.

In this exposition of the underlying concept I have had regard not only to the marks pertaining to the distinct cognition of the object, but somewhat also to the *two-fold* genesis of the concept from the nature of the mind, which, being serviceable to a method of deeper metaphysical insight, by way of example appears to me not a little commendable. For it is one thing, the parts being given, to conceive the *composition* of the whole by an abstract notion of the intellect, and another thing to *follow out* this general *notion* considered as a problem of the reason by the cognitive sensuous faculty, that is, to represent it to one's self in the concrete by a distinct intuition. The former is done through the class concept by *composition*, as several things are contained either under it or mutually, and hence by intellectual and universal ideas. The latter rests on the *conditions* of time, inasmuch as the concept of a composite is possible genetically, that is by *synthesis*, by the successive union of part to part, and falls under the laws of *intuition*. Similarly, a substantial composite being given, we easily attain to the idea of the simple parts by the general removal of the intellectual notion of *composition;* for what remains after the removal of conjunction are the simple parts. But according to the laws of intuitive cognition this is not done, that is, all composition is not removed, except by a regress from the given whole to *any possible parts* whatsoever—in other words, by an analysis again resting on the condition of time.[1] But since in order to a composite a *multiplicity*, in order to a whole, the *allness*, of parts is required, neither the analysis nor the synthesis will be complete; hence neither by the former will the concept of the *simple* part emerge, nor by the latter the concept of the *whole*, unless either can be gone through within a time that is finite and assignable.

But since in a *continuous quantity* the *regress* from the whole to assignable parts, and in an *infinite quantity* the *progress* from the parts to the given whole *are endless*, complete analysis in the one and complete synthesis in the other direction are impossible; hence neither the whole in the first

---

[1] To the words analysis and synthesis a two-fold meaning is commonly given; for the synthesis is either *qualitative*, a progress in a series of *subordinates* from the reason to the consequence, or *quantitative*, a progress in a series of co-ordinates from the given part through its complements to the whole. Similarly, analysis, taken in the first sense, is a regress from *the consequence to the reason,* but in the latter meaning a regress from a *whole* to its *possible* or mediate *parts,* that is, to the parts of parts; hence it is not a division but a *subdivision* of the given composite. Synthesis as well as analysis are here taken only in the latter sense.

case as to *composition*, nor the composite in the latter case as to *totality* can be thought completely in accordance with the laws of intuition. *Unthinkable* and *impossible* being vulgarly deemed to have the same meaning, it is plain why the concepts of the *continuous* as well as that of the *infinite* are rejected by most men as concepts whose representation *according to the laws of intuitive cognition* is impossible. Although I do not here champion these notions, especially not the first, which are considered exploded by many schools, still the following reminder is of the greatest moment. Those who use so perverse an argumentation have fallen into a grave error.[1] For whatever is repugnant to the laws of the intellect and reason is of course impossible, but that which being the object of pure reason does merely *not fall under* the laws of intuitive cognition is not so. For here the disagreement between the *sensuous* and the *intellectual* faculties, whose natures I shall presently explain, indicates nothing except *that the abstract ideas which the mind has received from the intellect can often not be followed out in the*

---

[1] Those who reject the actual mathematical infinite do not take much trouble. They frame a definition of the infinite from which they can shape out some contradiction. *The infinite* is said by them to be a *quantity than which none greater is possible*, and the mathematical infinite the multiplicity—of an assignable unit—than which none greater is possible. Having substituted *greatest* for *infinite* they easily conclude against an infinite of their own making, as a greatest multiplicity is impossible; or, they call an infinite multiplicity an *infinite number*, and show this to be absurd; which is plain enough, but a battle with their own fancy only. But if they would conceive of a mathematical infinite as a quantity which being referred to measure as unity is a multiplicity greater than all number; if, furthermore, they would take note that mensurability here denotes only the relation to the smallness of the human intellect, to which it is given to attain to a definite concept of multiplicity only by the successive addition of unit to unit, and to the sum total called number only by going through with this progress within a finite time, they would gain the clear insight that what does not fall in with a certain law of some subject does not on that account exceed all intellection; since an intellect may exist, though not a human one, perceiving a multiplicity distinctly by a single insight, without the successive application of measurement.

concrete and converted into intuitions. This *subjective* difficulty generally feigns some objective repugnance and easily deceives the incautious, the limits by which the human mind is circumscribed being taken for those by which the essence of things themselves is contained.

Furthermore, as the argument from intellectual reasonings easily shows that substantial composites being given, whether by the testimony of the senses or otherwise, the simple parts and the world are also given, so does our definition point out causes contained in the nature of the subject why the notion of a world should not seem merely arbitrary and made up, as in mathematics, only for the sake of the deducible consequences. The mind intent upon resolving as well as compounding the concept of a composite demands and presumes boundaries in which it may acquiesce in the former as well as in the latter direction.

Paragraph 2

In defining the World the following points require attention:

I. *Matter* (in the transcendental sense), that is, the *parts* which are here assumed to be *substances*. We might plainly be regardless of coincidence between our definition and the meaning of the common word, the question being, so to speak, of a problem arising in accordance with the laws of reasoning, namely, how several substances may coalesce into one, and on what condition rests this one's being no part of another. But the force of the word World, as commonly used, of itself falls in with us. For no one will attribute *accidents* to the *World* as *parts*, but as *determinations, states;* hence the so-called world of the *ego*, unrestrained by the single substance and its accidents, is not very appositely called a World, unless, perhaps, an imaginary one. For the same reason it is not permissible to refer the successive series—namely, of states—as a part to the mundane whole; for modifications are *not parts*, but *consequences* of the subject. Finally, as to the nature of the substances constituting the world, I have not here called into debate whether they be *contingent* or necessary, nor do I hide such a determination unproved in the definition in order subsequently, as is sometimes done, to draw it thence by some specious argumentation. But I shall show further on that their contingency can be amply concluded from the conditions here posited.

II. *Form*, which consists in the *co-ordination* of the substances, not in their subordination. For *co-ordinates* are to be regarded as mutual complements to a whole, *subordinates* as effect and cause, or generally, as principle and consequence. The former relation is reciprocal and *homonymous*, any correlate in respect to any other being considered as at once determining and determined. The latter is *heteronymous;* on the one hand dependence only, casuality on the other. This co-ordination is conceived as real and objective, not as ideal, and resting in the mere pleasure of a subject making up a whole by the summation of any multiplicity whatever. For the grasping of several things can by no contrivance be made a *whole of representation*, nor, for that reason, *a representation of the whole*. Therefore, if there be any totals of substances connected by no bond, a grasping of them together, the mind forcing the multiplicity into ideal oneness, will be called nothing more than a plurality of worlds comprehended in a single thought. But the connection constituting the *essential* form of a world is looked upon as the principle of the *possible influences* of the substances composing that world. For an actual influence pertains not to essence but to state, and the transitive forces, the causes of the influences, suppose some principle by which it is possible that the states of several things in other respects existing independently of each other are mutually related as consequences, which principle being abandoned, the possibility of transitive force in a world is an illicit assumption. And, furthermore, this *form essential* to the world is on that account *immutable*, and exposed to no vicissitude whatever. It is so in the first place for a logical reason, since any change supposes the identity of the subject with determinations succeeding one another in turn. Hence the world, remaining the same world through all the states succeeding one another, preserves the same fundamental form. For it does not suffice to the identity of the whole that all the *parts* be identical, the identity of characteristic *composition* is required also. But it follows especially from a *real cause*. For the nature of the world, which is the primary inner principle of whatever variable determinations may pertain to its state, never by any possibility being opposite to itself, is naturally, that is, by itself, immutable; hence there is given in any world whatever some form ascribable to its nature, constant and invariable, as the perennial principle of any contingent and transitory form pertaining to the state of the world. They who hold this disquisition superfluous are confuted by the concepts of space and time, conditions, as it were, given by their very own selves and primitive, by whose aid, that is to say, without any other principle, it is not only possible but necessary for several actual things to be regarded as reciprocally parts constituting a whole. But I shall show presently that these are plainly not *rational* notions, nor the bonds which they form objective *ideas*, but phenomena; and that though they witness, to be sure, some principle which is the common universal bond, it is not set forth by them.

III. *Universality*, which is the *absolute* allness of the appertaining parts. For, *regard* being had to any given composite, though it may be besides a part of another, still there always obtains a certain comparative allness, namely, that of the parts belonging to it as a particular quantity. But in this case whatsoever things are regarded as mutually parts of *whatsoever* whole, are understood to be conjointly posited. This absolute *totality*, apparently an everyday and perfectly obvious concept, especially when, as happens in the definition, it is enunciated negatively, when canvassed thoroughly becomes the crucial test of the philosopher. For it is scarce conceivable how the *inexhaustible series* of the states of the universe succeeding one another *eternally* be reducible to a *whole* comprehending all changes whatsoever. Since it is necessary to very infinitude to be without *end*, and hence no successive series is given but what is the part of another, completeness or *absolute totality* is by parity of reasoning plainly excluded. For although the notion of a part can be taken in a universal sense, and although everything contained under this notion, if regarded as posited in the same series, constitutes unity, yet the concept of the *whole* appears to exact their all being *taken simultaneously*, which in the case given is impossible. For, although to the whole series nothing succeeds, there is given in the succession no posited series to which nothing succeeds, unless it be the last. There will, then, in eternity be something which is last, which is absurd. Perhaps some may think that the difficulty which besets a successive infinite is absent from a *simultaneous infinite*, for the reason that apparently *simultaneity* plainly professes to embrace *all at the same time*. But, if the simultaneous infinite be admitted, the successive infinite also will have to be conceded, and the negation of the latter cancels the former. For the simultaneous infinite offers matters everlastingly inexhaustible to a successive progress in infinitum through its innumerable parts, which numberless series actually being given in the simultaneous infinite, a series though inexhaustible by successive addition could be given as a *whole*. In solution of the perplexing problem note;

that both the successive and the simultaneous co-ordination of several things, since they rest upon the concept of time, do not pertain to the *intellectual* concept of a whole, but only to the conditions of *sensuous intuition;* hence though not sensuously conceivable, they do not on that score cease being intellectual concepts. For in order to the latter it suffices that co-ordinates be given, no matter how, and that they be thought of as all pertaining to a unit.

SECTION II

ON THE DISTINCTION BETWEEN THE SENSIBLE AND THE INTELLIGIBLE GENERALLY

Paragraph 3

Sensibility is the *receptivity* of a subject by which it is possible for its representative state to be affected in a certain way by the presence of some object. *Intelligence*, rationality, is the *faculty* of a subject by which it is able to represent to itself what by its quality cannot enter the senses. The object of sensibility is sensuous; what contains nothing but what is knowable by the intellect is intelligible. In the older schools the former was called *phenomenon*, the latter *noumenon*. To the extent to which knowledge is subject to the laws of sensuousness it is sensuous; to the extent to which it is subject to the laws of intelligence it is *intellectual* or rational.

Paragraph 4

Since whatever is in sensuous knowledge depends upon the subject's peculiar nature, as the latter is capable of receiving some modification or other from the presence of objects which on account of subjective variety may be different in different subjects, whilst whatever knowledge is exempt from such subjective condition regards the object only, it is plain that what is sensuously thought is the representation of things *as they appear*, while the intellectual presentations are the representations of things *as they are.* Now there is in sense representation something which may be called the *matter*, namely, the *sensation*, and in addition to this something which may be called the *form*, namely, the *appearance* of the sensible things, showing forth to what extent a natural law of the mind co-ordinates the variety of sensuous affections. Furthermore, as the sensation constituting the *matter* of sensuous representations argues, to be sure, the presence of something sensible, but depends as to quality on the nature of the subject, as the latter is modifiable by the object; exactly so does the *form* of that representation witness certainly some reference or relation among the sensuous percepts, but itself is not, as it were, the shadowing forth or outlining of the object, but only a certain law inherent in the mind for co-ordinating among themselves sensuous percepts arising from the presence of the object. For by form or appearance the objects do not strike the sense, hence in order that various sense-affecting objects may coalesce iuto some whole of representation, there is need of an inner principle of the mind by which, in accordance with stable and innate laws, that variety shall take on some *appearance.*

Paragraph 5

To sensual cognition then pertains both the matter which is sensation and by which the knowledge is said to be *sensual*, and the form by which, even though we find it without any sensation, the representations are called *sensuous*. On the other hand, as to *intellectual* concepts, it is above all to be well noted that the use of the intellect, or of the superior faculty of the soul, is two-fold. By the first use are *given* the very concepts both of things and relations. This is the *real use*. By the second use they, whencesoever given, are merely by common marks *subordinated* to one another, the lower to the higher, and compared among themselves according to the principle of contradiction. This is called the *logical* use. The logical use of the intellect is common to all the sciences; the real use is not. For a cognition given in any wise is regarded either as contained under or as opposed to a mark common to several cognitions, and this either by immediate apposition, as in *judgments* in order to distinct cognition, or mediately, as in *reasoning*, in order to adequate cognition. Thus sensuous knowledge being given, sensuous percepts are by the logical use of the intellect subordinated to other sensuous percepts, as to common concepts, and phenomena to the more general laws of phenomena. In this connection it is of the greatest moment to note that cognitions must continue to be regarded as sensuous, no matter how great may have been the logical use of the intellect upon them. For they are called sensuous *on account of their origin*, not of their *collation* by identity and opposition. Hence, empirical laws, though of the greatest generality, are, nevertheless, sensual, and the principles of sensuous form in geometry, the relations in determinate space, however much the intellect arguing according to logical rules from what is sensuously given, by pure intuition, be employed upon them, do not for that matter pass beyond the class of sense-percepts. That in sense-percepts and phenomena which precedes the logical use of the intellect is called *appearance*, while the reflex knowledge originating from several appearances compared by the intellect is called *experience*. Thus there is no way from appearance to experience except by reflection according to the logical use of the intellect. The common concepts of experience are termed *empirical*, its objects *phenomena*, and the laws as well of experience as of all sensuous cognition generally are called the laws of phenomena. Empirical concepts, then, are not by a reduction to greater universality rendered intellectual in the *real sense* and do not transcend the species of sensuous cognition, but, however high abstraction may carry them, remain indefinitely sensuous.

Paragraph 6

Now as to *strictly intellectual concepts* in which the *use* of the *intellect* is *real*. Such concepts both of objects and relations are given by the very nature of the intellect, are not abstracted from any use of the senses, and do not contain any form of sensuous knowledge as such. It is needful here to take note of the extreme ambiguity of the word *abstract*, which, in order not to confuse our disquisition on intellectual concepts, must be removed to begin with, for properly we should say *abstract from some things*, not *abstract something*. The former denotes that in a concept we give no atention to other matters in whatsoever way they may be connected with it; but the latter, that it is not given but in the concrete and so as to be separated from what it is conjoined with. Hence an intellectual concept *abstracts* from everything sensuous, it is *not abstracted* from sensuous things, and perhaps would be more correctly called *abstracting* than *abstract*. Intellectual concepts it is more cautious, therefore, to call *pure ideas*, and concepts given only empirically, *abstract* ideas.

Paragraph 7

From the foregoing it will be seen that it is badly to expound the sensuous to call it the *more confusedly* known, and the intellectual the *distinctly* known. For these are only logical distictions and plainly do *not touch* the *data* underlying all logical comparison. The sensuous may be exceedingly distinct, while intellectual concepts are extremely confused. The former we observe in the prototype of sensuous knowledge, *geometry*; the latter, in the organon of all intellectual concepts, *metaphysics*. It is evident how much toil the latter is expending to dispel the fogs of confusion darkening the common intellect, though not always with the happy success of the former science. Nevertheless, any cognition retains the marks of its origin, the former, however distinct, being called by genesis sensuous; the latter, no matter how confused, remaining intellectual, as for instance, the *moral* concepts, which are known not experientially but by the pure intellect itself. The writer fears that Wolf by the distinction between the sensuous and the intellectual, which to him is only logical, checked, perhaps wholly, and to the great detriment of philosophy, that noble enterprise of antiquity of discussing the nature of phenomena and noumena, turning us from the investigation of these to what are frequently but logical trifles.

Paragraph 8

The *primary* philosophy containing the *principles* of the use *of pure intellect* is *metaphysics:* But there is a science *propaedeutical* to it, showing the distinction of sensuous cognition from intellectual, a specimen of which we present in this dissertation. Empirical principles not being found in metaphysics, the concepts to be met with in it are not then to be sought for in the senses, but in the very nature of pure intellect; not as *connate* notions, but as abstracted from laws whose seat is in the mind, by attending to the actions of the mind on the occasion of experience, and hence as *acquired*. Of this species are possibility, existence, necessity, substance, cause, etc., with their opposites and correlates, which, never entering as parts into any sensual representation, can by no means have been abstracted thence.

Paragraph 9

The purpose of intellectual concepts is mainly twofold; in the first place *refutative*, by which they are of negative use, when, shutting off sensuous concepts from noumena, though not advancing science a hair's breadth, they maintain however its immunity from the contagion of error. In the second place *dogmatic*, following which the general principles of pure intellect, such as are set forth in ontology or rational psychology, go forth into an exemplar inconceivable except by pure intellect, and the common measure of all other things considered as realities, namely, *noumenal perfection*. The latter is such either in the theoretical or in the practical sense.[1] In the former it is the highest being, *God*. In the latter sense, it is *moral perfection*. *Moral philosophy*, then, inasmuch as supplying the first *principles of judgment*, is not cognized except by pure intellect, and itself belongs to pure philosophy, and Epicurus reducing its criteria to deduction from the sense of pleasure or pain is rightly reprehended, together with some moderns following him a certain distance from afar, as Shaftesbury and his adherents. In any class of things having variable quantity the *maximum* is the common measure and the principle of cognition. Now the *maximum of perfection* is called *ideal*, by Plato, Idea—for instance, his Idea of a Republic—and is the principle of all that is contained under the general notion of any perfection, inasmuch as the lesser grades are not thought determinable but by limiting the maximum. But God, the Ideal of perfection, and hence the principle of cognition, is also, as existing really, the principle of the creation of all perfection.

Paragraph 10

To man, no *intuition* of intellectual concepts is given, only

[1] Something is considered theoretically when we attend only to what belongs to the thing; practically, when we view what by liberty should be in it.

symbolical cognition, and intellection is granted us only by universal concepts in the abstract, not by the concrete singular. For all intuition is restricted by some principle of form under which alone anything can be *discerned* by the mind immediately or as *singular*, and not merely conceived discursively by general concepts. This formal principle of our intuition—space and time—is the condition under which something can be an object of our senses, and hence as a condition of sensuous knowledge is not a medium for intellectual intuition. Besides, all the material of our cognition is given only by the senses, but the noumenon, as such, is not conceivable by representations drawn from sensations; hence the intellectual concept, as such, is destitute of all *data* of human intuition. For the intuition of our mind is always *passive*, and therefore possible only to the extent to which something can affect our senses. But the divine intuition, the cause—not the consequence, of objects, being independent, is the archetype, and hence perfectly intellectual.

Paragraph 11

But although phenomena are properly the appearances of things, but not ideas, or express the inner and absolute quality of objects, their cognition is nevertheless of the truest. For in the first place, being apprehended sensual concepts, they, being consequences, witness the presence of the object, contrary to Idealism; and as regards judgments concerning that which is sensuously known, since truth in judging consists in the agreement of the predicate with the given subject, and since the concept of the subject as a phenomenon is given only by relation to the sensuous cognitive faculty, the sensuously observable predicates being given according to the same, it is plain that the representations of subject and predicate are made according to common laws, and hence give occasion for perfectly true cognition.

Paragraph 12

All sense-objects are phenomena, but that which, not touching our senses, contains the form only of sensuality, belongs to pure intuition, that is, an intuition devoid of sensations, but not on that account, intellectual. Phenomena of the external sense are examined and set forth in *physics;* those of the internal sense in empirical psychology. But pure human intuition is not a universal or logical concept *under which*, but a singular *in which* all sensible objects are thought, and hence contains concepts of space and time, which, since they determine nothing concerning sensible objects as to *quality*, are not the objects of science except as to *quantity*. Hence *pure mathematics* considers *space* in *geometry* and *time* in *pure mechanics*. To these is to be added a certain concept, intellectual to be sure in itself, but whose becoming actual in the concrete requires the auxiliary notions of time and space in the successive addition and simultaneous juxtaposition of separate units, which is the concept of *number* treated in *arithmetic*. Pure mathematics, then, expounding the form of our entire sensuous cognition, is the organon of all intuitive and distinct knowledge, and since its objects are not only the formal principles of all intuition, but themselves original intuitions, it confers cognition both perfectly true, and the model of the highest degree of clearness to others. There is *given, therefore, a science of sensual things*, though being phenomena there is not given a real intellection, but a logical one only; hence it is plain in what sense those borrowing from the Eleatic school are to be thought to have denied a science of phenomena.

SECTION III

ON THE PRINCIPLES OF THE FORM OF THE SENSIBLE WORLD

Paragraph 13

The principle of the form of a universe is that which contains the cause of the universal tie by means of which all substances and their states pertain to one which is called a *world*. The principle of the form of the *sensible world* is that which contains the cause of the universal tie of all things regarded as *phenomena*. The form of the *intelligible world* acknowledges an objective principle, that is, some cause by which it is the colligation of what exists in it. But the world regarded as phenomenon, that is, in respect to the sensibility of the human mind, acknowledges no principle of form but a subjective one, that is, a certain mental law by which it is necessary that all things qualified for being objects of the senses would seem to pertain *necessarily* to the same whole. Whatever be, therefore, the principle of the form of the sensible world, it will comprise only *actual* things in as far as thought of as possibly falling under *sense-perception;* hence neither immaterial substances, which as such are excluded by definition from the external senses altogether, nor the cause of the world, which, since by it the mind exists and has the power of sense-perception, cannot be the object of the senses. These formal principles of the *phenomenal universe* which are absolutely primary, universal, and, so to speak, the outlines and conditions of anything else whatsoever in human sensuous cognition, I shall now show to be two: time and space.

Paragraph 14

OF TIME

1. *The idea of time does not originate in, but is presupposed by the senses.* Whether things falling under sense-perception be simultaneous or in line of succession cannot be represented but by the idea of time; nor does succession beget the concept of time; it appeals to it. Hence the notion of time, though acquired by experience, is badly defined by a series of actual things existing one *after* another, for what the word *after* means I understand only by the previous concept of time. For those things are *after* one another which exist at *different times*, as those are *simultaneous* which exist at the *same time*.

2. *The idea of time is singular*, not general. For any time whatever is thought only as a part of one and the same unmeasured time. If you think two years you cannot represent them to yourself but in a mutually determinate position, and if they do not immediately follow one the other, you cannot think of them except as connected by some intermediate time. Which of different times is *first* and which *later* can be defined in no way by any marks conceivable by the intellect, unless you are willing to run into a circle, and the mind discerns it by no more than one intuition. Besides, we conceive of all actual things as posited *in* time, not as contained as common marks *under* a general notion of time.

3. *The idea of time*, therefore, *is an intuition*, and being conceived before all sensation as the condition of the relations occurring in sensible things, it is not a sensual but *pure intuition*.

4. *Time is a continuous quantity* and the principle of the laws of continuity in the changes of the universe. For a *continuous* quantity is one which does not consist of simple

parts. But since by time are only thought relations without any mutually related data, there is in time—as a quantity—composition, which being conceived wholly removed leaves nothing over. But a composite of which, composition being removed, nothing is left, does not consist of simple parts. Therefore, etc. Any part of time, then, is time; and the simple things in time, namely, the *moments*, are not parts of it, but termini between which time intervenes. For two moments being given, time is not given, except as in them actualities succeed each other; hence, beside the given moment it is necessary that time be given in the latter part of which there is another moment.

The metaphysical law of *continuity* is this: *All changes are continuous* or flowing, that is, opposite states succeed each other only by an intermediate series of different states. For since two opposite states are in different moments of time, and some time is always intercepted between two moments, in which infinite series of moments the substance is neither in one assignable state nor the other, nor yet in none, it will be in different states, and so on infinitely.

The celebrated Kästner, calling in question this Leibnitzian law,[1] calls on its defenders to demonstrate that the *continuous motion of a point around the sides of a triangle is impossible*, it being necessary to prove this if the law of continuity be granted. Here is the demonstration required. Let the letters *a b c* denote the three angular points of a rectilineal triangle. If the point did move continuously over the lines *ab*, *bc*, *ca*, that is, over the perimeter of the figure, it would be necessary for it to move at the point *b* in the direction *ab*, and also at the same point *b* in the direction *bc*. These motions being diverse, they cannot be *simultaneous*. Therefore, the moment of presence of the movable point at vertex *b*, considered as moving in the direction *ab*, is different from

[1] Höhere Mechanik, p. 354.

the moment of presence of the movable point at the same vertex *b*, considered as moving in the same direction *bc*. But between two moments there is time; therefore, the movable point is present at point *b* for some time, that is, it *rests*. Therefore it does not move continuously, which is contrary to the assumption. The same demonstration is valid for motion over any right lines including an assignable angle. Hence a body does not change its direction in continuous motion except by following a line no part of which is straight, that is, a curve, as Leibnitz maintained.

5. *Time is not something objective and real*, neither a substance, nor an accident, nor a relation. It is the subjective condition necessary by the nature of the human mind for coordinating any sensible objects among themselves by a certain law; time is a *pure intuition*. Substances as well as accidents we co-ordinate whether according to simultaneity or succession by the concept only of time; hence the notion of time as the principle of form outranks the concepts of the former. Any relations so far as occurring in sense-perception, whether simultaneous or successive, involve nothing but the determination of positions in time, to wit, either in the same point or in different points of the latter.

Those who assert the objective reality of time either conceive of it as a continuous flow in what exists, without, however, any existing thing, as is done especially by the English philosophers, an absurd fiction, or as something real abstracted from the succession of inner states, as it has been put by Leibnitz and his followers. The falsity of the latter opinion, besides obviously exposing it to the vicious circle in the definition of time, and, moreover, plainly neglecting *simultaneity*, the most important consequence of time, disturbs all sound reason, because it demands instead of the determining of the laws of motion by the measure of time, that time itself, as to its nature, be determined by what is observed in motion or some series of inner changes, whereby plainly all certitude of rules is abolished. That we can estimate the *quantity* of time only in the concrete, namely, either by *motion* or by a *series of thoughts*, arises from the concept of time resting only on an inherent mental law, it not being a connate intuition; whence the act of the mind co-ordinating the impressions is elicited only by the aid of the senses. So far from its being possible to deduce and explain the concept of time from some other source by force of reason, it is presupposed by the very principle of contradiction, it underlies it by way of condition. For *a* and *not-a* are not repugnant unless thought of the *same thing simultaneously*, that is, at the same time; they may *belong* to the same thing *after* each other, at different times. Hence the possibility of changes is not thinkable except in time. Time is not thinkable by changes, but reversely.[1]

6. But although *time* posited in itself and absolutely be an imaginary thing, yet as appertaining to the immutable law of sensible things as such, it is a perfectly true concept, and the patent condition of intuitive representation throughout all the infinite range of possible sense-objects. For since simultaneous things as such cannot be placed before the senses but by the aid of time, and since changes are unthinkable except by time, it is obvious that this concept contains the univer-

[1] *Simultaneous facts* are not such for the reason that they do not succeed each other. Removing succession, to be sure, a conjunction is withdrawn which existed by the time-series. Yet thence does not originate *another* true relation, the conjunction of all things in the same moment. For simultaneous things are joined in the same moment of time exactly as successive things are joined in different moments. Hence, though time is of but one dimension, still the *ubiquity* of time, to speak with Newton, by which all things sensuously thinkable are *some time*, adds to the quantity of actual things another dimension, inasmuch as they hang, so to speak, on the same point of time. For designating time by a straight line produced infinitely, and the simultaneous things at any point of time whatever by lines applied in succession, the surface thus generated will represent the *phenomenal world*, both as to substance and accidents.

sal form of phenomena, and that, indeed, all events observable in the world, all motions, all internal changes, agree necessarily with the temporal axioms of cognition which we have partly expounded, *since only under these conditions can they become sense-objects and be co-ordinated.* It is, therefore, absurd to excite reason against the primary postulates of pure time, as, for example, continuity, etc., since they follow from laws prior and superior to which nothing is found, and since reason herself in the use of the principle of contradiction cannot dispense with the support of this concept, so primitive and original is it.

7. Time, then, is the absolutely first *formal principle of the sensible world.* For all sensible things of whatsoever description are unthinkable except as posited either simultaneously or one after another, and, indeed, as if involved and mutually related by determinate position in the tract of unique time, so that by this primary concept of everything sensuous originates necessarily that formal whole which is not a part of another, that is, the *phenomenal World.*

Paragraph 15

OF SPACE

A. *The concept of space is not abstracted from external sensations.* For I am unable to conceive of anything posited without me unless by representing it as in a place different from that in which I am, and of things as mutually outside of each other unless by locating them in different places in space. Therefore the possibility of external perceptions, as such, *presupposes* and does not *create* the concept of space, so that, although what is in space affects the senses, space cannot itself be derived from the senses.

B. *The concept of space is a singular representation* comprehending all things *in itself,* not an abstract and common notion containing them *under* itself. What are called *several spaces* are only parts of the same immense space mutually related by certain positions, nor can you conceive of a cubic foot except as being bounded in all directions by surrounding space.

C. *The concept of space, therefore, is a pure intuition*, being a singular concept, not made up by sensations, but itself the fundamental form of all external sensation. This pure intuition is in fact easily perceived in geometrical axioms, and any mental construction of postulates or even problems. That in space there are no more than three dimensions, that between two points there is but one strainght line, that in a plane surface from a given point with a given right line a circle is describable, are not conclusions from some universal notion of space, but only *discernible* in space as in the concrete. Which things in a given space lie toward one side and which are turned toward the other can by no acuteness of reasoning be described discursively or reduced to intellectual marks. There being in perfectly similar and equal but incongruous solids, such as the right and the left hand, conceived of solely as to extent, or spherical triangles in opposite hemispheres, a difference rendering impossible the coincidence of their limits of extension, although for all that can be stated in marks intelligible to the mind by speech they are interchangeable, it is patent that only by pure intuition can the difference, namely, incongruity, be noticed. Geometry, therefore, uses principles not only undoubted and discursive but falling under the mental view, and the *obviousness* of its demonstrations—which means the clearness of certain cognition in as far as assimilated to sensual knowledge—is not only greatest, but the only one which is given in the pure sciences, and the *exemplar* and medium of all *obviousness* in the others. For, since geometry considers the *relations of space*, the concept of which contains the very form of all sensual intuition, nothing that is perceived by the external sense can be clear and perspicuous unless by means of that intuition which it is the business of geometry to contemplate. Besides, this science does not demonstrate its universal propositions by thinking the object through the universal concept, as is done in intellectual disquisition, but by submitting it to the eyes in a single intuition, as is done in matters of sense.[1]

D. *Space is not something objective* and real, neither substance, nor accident, nor relation; but *subjective* and ideal, arising by fixed law from the nature of the mind like an outline for the mutual co-ordination of all external sensations whatsoever. Those who defend the reality of space either conceive of it as an *absolute* and immense *receptacle* of possible things, an opinion which, besides the English, pleases most geometricians, or they contend for its being the relation of existing things *itself*, which clearly vanishes in the removal of things and is thinkable only in actual things, as besides Leibnitz, is maintained by most of our countrymen. The first inane fiction of the reason, imagining true infinite relation without any mutually related things, pertains to the world of fable. But the adherents of the second opinion fall into a much worse error. Whilst the former only cast an obstacle in the way of some rational or noumenal concepts, otherwise most recondite, such as questions concerning the spiritual world, omnipresence, etc., the latter place themselves in flat opposition to the very phenomena, and to the most faithful interpreter of all phenomena, to geometry.

---

[1] As the necessity of conceiving space as a continuous quantity is easy to demonstrate, I pass it by. It is a consequence from this that the simple in space is not a part, but a limit. A limit generally, is that in a continuous quantity which contains the limited portion. Space not the limit of another is a solid. The limit of a solid is a surface, of a surface the line, of a line the point; hence there are three kinds of limits in space, as there are three dimensions. Two of these limits, the surface and the line, are themselves spaces. The concept of limit enters into no quantity besides time and space.

For, not to enlarge upon the obvious circle in which they become involved in defining space, they cast forth geometry, thrown down from the pinnacle of certitude, into the number of those sciences whose principles are empirical. If we have obtained all the properties of space by experience from external relations only, geometrical axioms have only comparative universality, such as is acquired by induction. They have universality evident as far as observed, but neither necessity, except as far as the laws of nature may be established, nor precision, except what is arbitrarily made. There is hope, as in empirical sciences, that a space may some time be discovered endowed with other primary properties, perchance even a rectilinear figure of two lines.

E. Though the *concept of space* as an objective and real thing or quality is imaginary, it is nevertheless *in respect to all sensible things* not only *perfectly true*, it is the foundation of truth in external sensibility. Things cannot appear to the senses under any form but by means of a power of the soul co-ordinating all sensations in accordance with a fixed law implanted in its nature. Since, therefore, nothing at all can be given the senses except conformably to the primary axioms of space and their consequences which are taught by geometry, though their principle be but subjective, yet the soul will necessarily agree with them, since to this extent it agrees with itself; and the laws of sensuality will be the laws of nature *so far as it can be perceived by our senses*. Nature, therefore, is subject with absolute precision to all the precepts of geometry as to all the properties of space there demonstrated, this being the subjective condition, not hypothetically but intuitively given, of every phenomenon in which nature can ever be revealed to the senses. Surely, unless the concept of space were originally given by the nature of the mind, so as to cause him to toil in vain who should labor to fashion mentally any relations other than those prescribed by it, since in the fiction he would be compelled to employ the aid of this very same concept, geometry could not be used very safely in natural philosophy. For it might be doubted whether this same notion drawn from experience would agree sufficiently with nature, the determinations from which it was abstracted being, perchance, denied, a suspicion of which has entered some minds already. *Space*, then, is the absolutely first *formal principle of the sensible world*, not only because by its concept the objects of the universe can be phenomena, but especially for the reason that it is essentially but one, comprising all externally sensible things whatsoever; and hence constitutes the principle of the *universe*, that is, of that whole which cannot be the part of another.

COROLLARY

Here, then, are *two principles of sensuous cognition*, not, as in intellectual knowledge, general concepts, but *single and nevertheless pure intuition*, in which the parts, and especially the simple parts, do not, as the laws of reason prescribe, contain the possibility of the composite, but, according to the pattern of sensuous intuition, the *infinite* contains the reason of the part, and finally of its thinkable simple part or rather limit. For unless infinite space as well as infinite time be given, no definite space and time is assignable *by limitation*, and a point as well as a moment is unthinkable by itself and only conceived in a space and time already given as the limits. All primitive properties of these concepts are then beyond the purview of reason, and hence cannot intellectually be explained in any way. Nevertheless, they are *what underlies the intellect* when from intuitive primary data it derives consequences according to logical laws with the greatest possible certainty. *One* of these concepts properly concerns the intuition of the *object;* the other the *state*, especially the *representative* state. Hence space is employed as the type even of the concept of *time* itself, representing it by a line, and its limits—moments—by points. Time, on the other had, *approaches* more to a *universal* and *rational concept*, comprising under its relations all things whatsoever, to wit, space itself, and besides, those accidents which are not comprehended in the relations of space, such as the thoughts of the soul. Again, time, besides this, though it certainly does not dictate the laws of reason, yet *constitutes* the principal *conditions under* favor of *which the mind compares its notions according to the laws of reason.* Thus, I cannot judge what is impossible except by predicating *a* and *not-a* of the same subject *at the same time.* And especially, considering experience, though the reference of cause to effect in external objects were to lack the relations of space, still in all things, external or internal, the mind could by the auxiliary relation of time alone be informed which is the first and which latter or caused. And even the *quantity* of space itself cannot be rendered intelligible unless, referring it to measure as to a unity, we set it forth in number, which itself is but multiplicity distinctly cognized by numeration, that is, by the successive addition of one to one in a given time.

Lastly, the question will arise in any one as if spontaneously, whether either *concept* be *connate* or *acquired*. The latter by what has been shown seems refuted already, but the former, smoothing the way for *lazy philosophy*, declaring vain by the citing of a first cause any further quest, is not to be admitted thus rashly. But beyond doubt *either concept is acquired*, not, it is true, abstracted from the sense of objects, for sensation gives the matter not the form of human cognition, but from the very action of the mind co-ordinating its sense-percepts in accordance with perpetual laws, as though an immutable type, and hence to be known intuitively. For sensations excite this act of the mind but do not influence intuition, neither is there anything connate here except the law of the soul in accordance with which it conjoins in a certain way its sensations derived from the presence of an object.

SECTION IV

ON THE PRINCIPLE OF THE FORM OF THE INTELLIGIBLE WORLD

Paragraph 16

Those who deem space and time to be something real and the absolute bond, so to speak, of all possible substances in space, hold nothing else to be required in order to conceive how an original relation can belong to several existing things as the primitive condition of possible influence and the principle of the essential form of the universe. For since whatever exists is, according to their opinion, necessarily somewhere, it seems to them quite superfluous to inquire why things are present to one another in a certain manner, since this is of itself determined by the universality of all-comprehending space. But this concept, besides relating as has been shown rather to the sensuous laws of the subject than to the conditions of the objects themselves, even granting it the greatest reality, still denotes nothing but the intuitively given possibility of universal co-ordination, leaving undealt with the question solvable only by the intellect: *In what principle does this very relation of all substances rest, which intuitively regarded is called space?* The question of the *principle of the form of the intelligible world* turns, therefore, upon making apparent in what manner it is possible *for several substances to be in mutual commerce,* and for this reason to pertain to the same whole, which is called world. We do not here consider the world, let it be understood, as to matter, that is, as to the nature of the substances of which it consists, whether they be material or immaterial, but as to form, that is to say, how among several things taken separately a connection, and among them all, totality can have place.

Paragraph 17

Several substances being given, the *principle* of their possible *intercommunication is not apparent from their existence solely*, but something else is required besides from which their mutual relations may be understood. For on account of mere existence they are not necessarily related to anything, unless it be to their cause; but the relation of an effect to the cause is not intercommunication, but dependence. Therefore, if any commerce intervenes among them, there is need of an exactly determining specific reason.

The sham cause in *physical influence* consists in rashly assuming that the commerce of substance and transitive forces is sufficiently knowable from their mere existence. Hence it is not so much a system as rather the neglect of all philosophical system as a superfluity in the argument. Freeing the concept from this defect, we shall have a species of commerce alone deserving to be called real, and from which the whole constituting the world merits being called real, and not ideal or imaginary.

Paragraph 18

A whole from necessary substances is impossible. For, since the existence of each stands for itself without dependence on any other, a dependence which in necessary substances clearly cannot befall, it is plain that not only does the intercommunication of substances (that is, the reciprocal dependence of their states) not follow from their existence, but as necessary substances cannot belong to them at all.

Paragraph 19

The whole, therefore, of substances is a whole of contingent things, and the *world consists essentially of only contingent things*. Besides, no necessary substance is in connection with the world except as a cause with the effect, and, therefore, not as a part with its complements making up a whole, since the bond connecting parts is mutual dependence, which in a necessary being cannot occur. The cause, therefore, of the world is an extramundane being, and so is not the soul of the world, nor is its presence in the world local, but virtual.

Paragraph 20

The mundane substances are beings from another being; not from several, but *all from one*. For, suppose them to be caused by several necessary beings. In intercommunication there are not effects from causes alien to all mutual relation. Hence, the *unity* in the *conjunction of the substances of the universe is the consequence of the dependence of all on one*. Therefore, the form of the universe witnesses the cause of matter, and only the *sole cause of all things is the cause of the universe*, nor is there an *architect* of the world not at the same time its *creator*.

Paragraph 21

If there were several primary and necessary causes together with their effects, their works would be *worlds*, not a *world*, since they would in no wise be connected into one whole. And vice versa, if there be several actual worlds without one another, several primary and necessary causes are given, so, however, as to give intercommunication neither to one world with another, nor to the cause of one with the world caused by another.

Several actual worlds without one another *are not,* therefore, *impossible by the very concept*, as Wolf hastily concluded from the notion of a complex or multiplicity which he deemed sufficient to a whole, as such, but only on condition *that there exist but one necessary cause of all things*. If several are admitted, *several worlds without one another will be possible* in the strictest metaphysical sense.

Paragraph 22

If, as we validly conclude from a given world to a single cause of all its parts, we may similarly argue reversely from the given cause common to all to their interconnection, and hence to the form of the world—though I confess this conclusion does not seem as plain to me—then the primary connection of substances will not be contingent but *by the sustentation* of all *by the common principle*, necessary, and hence the harmony proceeding from their very subsistence founded in a common cause would proceed according to the usual rules. Such a *harmony* I term *established generally;* as that which does not take place except as far as any individual states of a substance are adapted to the condition of another is *harmony established particularly;* the communion by the former being real and *physical*, by the latter ideal and *sympathetic*. All communion, then, of the substance of the universe is *eternally established* by the common cause of all, and either established generally by physical influence—as amended; see paragraph 17—or adapted particularly to their states; and the latter either rests *originally* in the primary constitution of every substance or is impressed on the *occasion* of any change whatever; the first being called *pre-established harmony*, the latter *occasionalism*. If, then, on account of the sustentation of all substances by one, the *conjunction* of all constituting them a unit be *necessary*, the universal commerce of substances will be by *physical influence*, and the world a real whole; if not, the commerce will be sympathetic, that is a harmony without true commerce, and the world only an ideal whole. To me the former, though not demonstrated, appears abundantly proved by other reasons.

SCHOLIUM

If it were right to overstep a little the limits of apodictic certainty befitting metaphysics, it would seem worth while to trace out some things pertaining not merely to the laws but even to the causes of sensuous intuition, which are only *intellectually* knowable. Of course the human mind is not affected by external things, and the world does not lie open to its insight infinitely, except *as far as itself together with all other things is sustained by the same infinite power of one.* Hence it does not perceive external things but by the presence of the same common sustaining cause; and hence space, which is the universal and necessary condition of the joint presence of everything known sensuously, may be called the *phenomenal omnipresence,* for the cause of the universe is not present to all things and everything, as being in their places, but their places, that is the relations of the substances, are possible, because it is intimately present to all. Furthermore, since the possibility of the changes and successions of all things whose principle as far as sensuously known resides in the concept of time, supposes the continuous existence of the subject whose opposite states succeed; that whose states are in flux, lasting not, however, unless sustained by another; the concept of time as one infinite and immutable in which all things are and last, is the *phenomenal eternity* of the general *cause.*[1] But it seems more cautious to hug the shore of the cognitions granted to us by the mediocrity of our intellect than to

---

[1] The moments of time do not appear to follow one another, since if they did another time would have to be premised for the succession of moments; but by sensuous intuition the actual things appear to descend, as it were, through a continuous series of moments.

be carried out upon the high seas of such mystic investigations, like Malebranche, whose opinion that *we see all things in God* is pretty nearly what has here been expounded.

SECTION V

ON THE METHOD RESPECTING THE SENSUOUS AND THE INTELLECTUAL IN METAPHYSICS

Paragraph 23

In all sciences whose principles are given intuitively, whether by sensual intuition, that is, experience, or by an intuition sensuous, to be sure, but pure—the concepts of space, time, and number—that is to say, in the natural and in the mathematical sciences, *use gives method*, and by trying and finding after the science has been carried to some degree of copiousness and consonancy it appears by what method and in what direction we must proceed in order to finish and to purify it by removing the defects of error as well as of confused thoughts; exactly as grammar after the more copious use of speech, and style after the appearance of choice examples in poetry and oratory, furnished vantage-ground to rules and to discipline. But the *use of the intellect* in the sciences whose primitive concepts as well as axioms are given by sensuous intuition is only *logical*, that is, by it we only subordinate cognitions to one another according to their relative universality conformably to the principle of contradiction, phenomena to more general phenomena, and consequences of pure intuition to intuitive axioms. But in pure philosophy, such as metaphysics, in which the *use of the intellect* in respect to principles is *real*, that is to say, where the primary concept of things and relations and the very axioms are given originally by the pure intellect itself, and not being intuitions do not enjoy immunity from error, *the method precedes the whole science,* and whatever is attempted before its precepts are thoroughly discussed and firmly established is looked upon as rashly conceived and to be rejected among vain instances of mental playfulness. For, since here the right use of the reason constitutes the very principles and the objects as well, what axioms are to be thought of concerning them become primarily known solely by its own nature, the exposition of the laws of pure reason is the very origin of the science, and their distinction from spurious laws the criterion of truth. The method of the science not being practiced much nowadays, except what logic prescribes to all sciences generally, that fitted for the peculiar nature of metaphysics being simply ignored, it is no wonder that those who everlastingly turn the Sisyphean stone of this inquiry do not seem so far to have made much progress. Though here I neither can nor will expatiate upon so important and extensive a subject, I shall briefly shadow forth what constitutes no despicable part of this method, namely, the *infection between sensuous and intellectual cognition,* not only as creeping in on those incautious in the application of principles, but even producing spurious principles under the appearance of axioms.

Paragraph 24

In substance the whole method of metaphysics as to the sensuous and the intellectual amounts to this precept; to take care *not to allow the principles at home in sensuous cognition to outstray their limits and affect the intellectual concepts.* For, since the *predicate* in any judgment enounced intellectually *is a condition* in the absence of which the subject is asserted to be unthinkable, the predicate hence being the principle of cognition, it will, if a sensuous concept, be only the condition of a possible sensuous cognition—and hence will square well enough with the subject of a judgment whose concept is also sensuous. But if it be applied to an intellectual concept, the judgment will be valid only according to subjective laws, and hence must not be affirmed objectively and predicated of the intellectual notion itself, but *only as a condition in the absence of which the sensuous cognition of the given concept does not take place*.[1]

Now, since the tricks of the intellect by the subordination of sensuous concepts as though intellectual marks may be called, analogously to the accepted meaning, *a fallacy of subreption*, the exchanging of intellectual and sensual concepts will be a *metaphysical fallacy of subreption*, the *intellectualized phenomenon*, if the barbarous expression be permissible, and hence I call such a *hybrid* axiom as palms off the sensuous as necessarily adhering to the intellectual concept, a *surreptitious axiom*. From these spurious axioms have gone forth, and are rife throughout metaphysics, principles deceiving the intellect. In order that we may have, however, a readily and clearly knowable citerion of those judgments, a touchstone, so to speak, by which to distinguish them from genuine judgments, and at the same time if, perhaps, they seem to cling tenaciously to the intellect, an

---

[1] The use of this criterion is fruitful and easy in distinguishing principles which enunciate laws of sensuous cognition only from those prescribing besides something concerning the objects themselves. If the predicate be an intellectual concept, its reference to the subject of the judgment, though this subject be thought of as an object of sense, always denotes a mark belonging to the object itself. *If the predicate be a sensuous concept*, then, since the laws of sensuous cognition are not conditions of the possibility of things themselves, it is not valid as to the *subject* of the judgment *conceived intellectually*, and hence it cannot be enounced objectively. Thus in the common axiom *whatever exists is somewhere*, as the predicate contains conditions of sensuous knowledge it cannot be enounced as to the subject of the judgment, namely, anything *existing*, generally; hence this formula as an objective rule is false. But converting the proposition, so as to make the predicate an intellectual concept, it becomes perfectly true; thus: whatever is somewhere, exists.

assaying art by which we can justly estimate how much belongs to the sensuous and how much to the intellectual sphere, I lhink it necessary to go into the question more deeply.

Paragraph 25

Here, then, is the *principle of reduction* for any spurious axiom: *If concerning any intellectual concept something pertaining to time and space relations be predicted generally, it is not to be enounced objectively, but denotes only the condition without which the given concept is not knowable sensuously.* That such an axiom is spurious, and, if not false, at least a rash and question-begging assertion, appears thus: the subject of the judgment being intellectually conceived pertains to the object, whilst the predicate, since it contains the determinations of space and time, pertains only to the conditions of human sensuous cognition, which, not adhering of necessity to any cognition whatsoever of the object, cannot be enounced concerning the given intellectual concept universally. The intellect's being so readily subject to this fallacy of subreption comes of its being deceived under the plea of another and perfectly true rule. For we rightly suppose that *that which can be cognized by no intuition whatever is utterly unthinkable* and hence impossible. But since we cannot attain by any mental striving, even fictitiously, to any other intuition but that according to the form of space and time, it happens that we deem all intuition whatever impossible which is not bound by these laws, passing by the pure intellectual intuition exempt from the laws of the senses, such as the divine, by Plato called the Idea, and hence subject all possible given things to the sensual axioms of space and time.

Paragraph 26

All sleights of substitution of sensuous cognition under

guise of intellectual concepts, from which spurious axioms originate, can be reduced to three species, whose general formulæ are the following:

1. The sensual condition under which alone the *intuition* of an object is possible, is the condition of its *possibility*.

2. The sensual condition under which alone *data can be compared in order to form the intellectual concept of the object*, is the condition of the very possibility of the object.

3. The sensual condition under which alone the *subsumption* of an *object under a given intellectual concept is possible, is the condition of the possibiltty of the object.*

Paragraph 27

A spurious axiom of the *first class* is: *Whatever is, is somewhere and sometime*.[1] Now by this spurious principle all beings, even though they be intellectually cognized, are restricted in existence by the conditions of space and time. Hence people discuss all sorts of inane questions, such as concerning the places of immaterial substances—of which, for that very reason, there is no sensuous intuition, nor, under that form, any representation—in the corporeal universe, or the seat of the soul; and as they improperly mix sensual things with intellectual concepts, like square figures with round, it oftens happens that of the disputants one appears as milking a he-goat, and the other as holding the sieve under. The presence of immaterial substances in the cor-

[1] Space and time are conceived as comprehending in *them* all things in any way offered to the senses. Hence, according to the laws of the human mind, the intuition of nothing is given except as contained in *space and time*. To this prejudice another may be compared which is not properly a spurious axiom but a play of the fancy, and which may be set forth in the general formula: In whatever exists *are space and time*, that is to say, every substance is *extended* and continuously *changed*. But though people of dense conception are bound firmly by this law of imagination, even they see readily that it pertains only to the efforts of fancy, shadowing forth to itself the appearance of things, not to the conditions of existence.

poreal world is virtual, not local, though thus improperly talked about. Space does not contain the conditions of possible mutual activities, except those of matter. What may constitute the external relations of forces in immaterial substances, as well among themselves as toward bodies, altogether escapes the human intellect, as was acutely noted, for instance, in a letter to a German prince by the clear-sighted Euler, otherwise a great investigator and judge of phenomena. But when people have arrived at the concept of a highest and extra-mundane being, they are fooled by these shadows flitting before the intellect to a degree beyond the force of language to express. The presence of God they figure to themselves as a *local* one, involving God in the world as if also comprised in infinite space, compensating Him for this limitation by a locality, so to speak, *eminently* conceived, that is, infinite. But it is absolutely impossible to be at the same time in several places, since different places are mutually without each other, and hence what is in several places is outside of itself, which implies being present to itself externally. But as to time, having not only exempted it from the laws of sensual knowledge, but transferred it beyond the limits of the world to the extra-mundane Being Himself as a condition of His existence, they involve themselves in an inextricable labyrinth. Hence they cudgel their brains with absurd questions, such as, for instance, why God did not make the world many centuries earlier. They persuade themselves that it is easy to conceive, to be sure, how God may discern what is present, that is, what is actual in the *time in which he is*, but how He may foresee what is future, that is, what is actual in the *time in which He is not yet*, they deem an intellectual difficulty; as if the existence of the Necessary Being descended through all the moments of an imaginary time, and, having already exhausted a part of His duration, saw before Him the eternity He was yet to live simultaneously with the present events of the world. All these difficulties upon proper insight into the notion of time vanish like smoke.

Paragraph 28

The prejudices of the second species, since they impose upon the intellect by the sensual conditions restricting the mind if it wishes in certain cases to attain to what is intellectual, lurk more deeply. One of them is that which affects knowledge of quantity, the other that affecting knowledge of qualities generally. The former is: *every actual multiplicity can be given numerically*, and hence, every infinite quantity; the latter, *whatever is impossible contradicts itself*. In either of them the concept of time, it is true, does not enter into the very notion of the predicate, nor is it attributed as a qualification to the subject. But yet it serves as a means for forming an idea of the predicate, and thus, being a condition, affects the intellectual concept of the subject to the extent that the latter is only attained by its aid.

As to the *first*, as every quantity and any series whatever are distinctly known only by successive co-ordination, the intellectual concept of amount and multiplicity arises only by the aid of this concept of time, and never attains to completeness unless the synthesis can be gone through with in finite time. It is hence that the *infinite series* of co-ordinate things cannot be comprehended distinctly according to the limits of our intellect; it hence by the fallacy of subreption seems impossible. According to the laws of pure intellect any series of effects has its *principle*, that is, there is not given in a series of effects a regress without a limit; whilst according to sensual laws any series of co-ordinate things has its assignable *beginning*. These propositions, the latter of which involves the *mensurability* of the series, the former the *dependence* of the whole, are taken hastily for identical.

In the same way, to the *argument of the intellect*, proving that a substantial composite being given so are the elements of composition, that is, the simple things, there is adjoined a *supposititious* one suborned from sensual knowledge, namely, that in such a composite there is not given an infinite regress in the composition of the parts, that is to say, that in any composite there is given a definite number of parts, a sense certainly not germane to the former, and hence substituted rashly for it. For that the quantity of the world is limited, not the maximum, that it owns a principle, that bodies consist of simple parts, can certainly be cognized rationally. But that the universe as to its mass is mathematically finite, that its age as elapsed can be given by measure, that the number of simple parts constituting any body whatever is a definite number, are propositions openly proclaiming their origin from the nature of sensual knowledge; however true they may be held to be, they bear the undoubted stigma of their origin.

As for the *latter spurions axiom*, it originates from a rash conversion of the principle of contradiction. For to this primitive judgment the concept of time adheres to the extent that contradictorily opposed data being given *at the same time* in the same thing, the impossibility is plain, which is enounced thus: *whatever stimultaneously is and is not, is impossible*. Here, as the intellect predicates something in a case given according to sensual laws, the judgment is perfectly true and obvious. On the contrary, converting this axiom, saying: *whatever is impossible is and is not at the same time*, or involves a contradiction, we predicate through sensual knowledge something concerning the object of reason generally, thus subjecting the intellectual conception of the possible and the impossible to the conditions of sensual knowledge, namely, to the relations of time; which certainly is true enough of the laws restricting and limiting the human intellect, but cannot be conceded objectively and generally by any means. Of course, our intellect *perceives no impossibility* except where it can note the simultaneous enunciation of opposites concerning the same thing, that is, only where contradiction occurs. Wherever, therefore, this contradiction does not occur, there is no room for the judgment of impossibility by the human intellect. But that on this account it should be open to no intellect whatever, and hence that *what does not involve contradiction is therefore possible*, is concluded rashly by taking the subjective conditions of judgment for objective ones. It is for this reason that a host of fictitious *forces*, gotten up *ad libitum*, bursts, in the absence of self-contradiction, from any constructive, or, if you prefer, from every chimerical mind. For as a *force* is nothing but a *relation* of a substance *a* to *something else b*, an accident, as of a reason to the consequence, the possibility of any force does *not rest in the identity* of the cause and the effect, or the substance and the accident, and hence even the impossibility of forces made up falsely does *not depend solely on contradiction*. Therefore it is not permissible to assume as possible any *original force* unless the force be *given by experience*. Neither can the possibility be conceived *a priori* by any perspicacity of the intellect.

Paragraph 29

The spurious axioms of the *third* kind from conditions proper to the *subject* whence they are transferred rashly to the *object* are plentiful, not, as in those of the Second Class, because the only way to the intellectual concept lies *through the sensuous data*, but because only by aid of the latter can the concept *be applied* to that which is *given* by experience, that is, can we know whether something is contained under a certain intellectual concept or not. To this class belongs the threadbare one of the schools: *whatever exists contingently does at some time not exist*. This spurious principle springs from the poverty of the intellect, having insight frequently into the *nominal*, rarely into the *real*, marks of contingency or necessity. Hence, whether the opposite of any substance be possible, an insight hardly obtained from *a priori* marks, is not otherwise known than by its being evident *that at some time that substance was not;* and changes rather witness contingency than contingency mutability, so that were nothing fleeting and transitory to occur in the world, a notion of contingence would hardly be possible in us. Therefore, though the direct proposition is perfectly true: *whatever at some time was not is contingent*, its converse indicates nothing but the conditions under which we can alone distinguish whether something exists necessarily or contingently. Hence if enunciated as a subjective law, which indeed it is, it should be enounced thus: *Sufficient marks of contingency of that of which it is not evident that at some time it was not, are not, by common intelligence, given.* This, however, tacitly deviates into an objective condition, as though in its absence there were no room for contingence; which being done, a counterfeit and erroneous axiom arises. For this world though existing contingently *is sempiternal*, that is, simultaneous with all time. It is a rash assertion that there was a time when it did not exist.

Paragraph 30

To these spurious principles must be added some others of great affinity with them, not imparting to the given intellectual concept any blemish of sensuous cognition, but deceiving the intellect so as to take them for arguments drawn from the object, though they are commended to us only by the peculiar nature of the intellect *for the convenience* of its free and ample use. Therefore, these as well as those enumerated above, rest in *subjective* reasons, although not in the laws of sensuous, but in those of intellectual cognition itself, namely, in the conditions under which it appears easy and quick to the mind to make use of its insight. I shall beg leave to throw in here, by way of conclusion, some mention of these principles, not as yet, as far as I know, set forth distinctly. I call, then, *principles of convenience* rules of judging to which we freely submit, and to which we adhere as if they were axioms, for the only reason that, *were we to depart from them, scarcely any judgment concerning a given object would be permissible to our intellect.* In this list belong the following: *First*, that by which we assume that *everything in the universe is done according to the order of nature*, which principle by Epicurus was proclaimed without any restriction, and by all other philosophers unanimously with extremely rare exceptions, not to be admitted but from supreme necessity. Still we thus affirm, not on account of possessing so ample a knowledge of the events of the world according to the common laws of nature, or because the impossibility or smaller hypothetical possiblity of supernatural things is plain to us, but because departing from the order of nature there would be no use for the intellect, the rash citation of the supernatural being the couch of lazy understandings. For the same reason we take care to shut out from the exposition of phenomena *comparative miracles*, namely, the influence of spirits, since, as we do not know their nature, the intellect, to its great detriment, would be turned aside from the light of experience, by which alone it is able to provide for itself laws of judging, into the night of species and causes unknown to us. The *second is the partiality for unity* proper to the philosophical mind, whence this wide-spread canon has flown forth: *principles are not to be multiplied beyond supreme necessity*, to which we give in our adhesion, not because we have insight into causal unity in the world either by reason or experience, but as seeking it by an impulse of the intellect which seems to itself to have by thus much advanced in the explication of phenomena, by as much as it is granted to it to descend from the same principle to a greater number of consequences, The *third* of this kind of principles is: *matter neither originates nor perishes;* all the changes in the world concern *form* only; a postulate which on the recommendation of common sense has spread through all philosophical schools, not because it is to be taken as having been found so, or as having been demonstrated by arguments *a priori*, but because if we were to admit that matter itself is fleeting and transitory, nothing at all that is stable and lasting would be left any longer to serve for the explication of phenomena according to universal and perpetual laws, and hence nothing at all would be left for the exercise of the intellect.

This method, especially in respect to the distinction between sensual and intellectual knowledge, which, when reduced by more careful investigation to exactness, will occupy the position of a propaedeutical science, will certainly be of unlimited benefit to all intending to penetrate into the very recesses of metaphysics.

NOTE.—As in this last section the tracing out of the method occupies all the space at disposal, and the rules prescribing the true form of arguing concerning sensuous things shine by their own light and do not borrow it from the illustrative examples, I have thrown in but a cursory mention of the latter. For this reason it is not strange if some things should seem to have been asserted with more audacity than truth, they certainly calling, when a broader treatment shall be possible, for greater force of arguments. Thus, what is alleged in paragraph 27 on the locality of immaterial substances lacks an explication which, if the reader please, may be found in Euler in the place cited, Vol. II, pp. 49, 52. For the soul *is* not in communion with the body as being detained in a certain place in the latter, but a determined place in the universe is attributed to it, for the reason that it is in mutual commerce with some body, which commerce being dissolved all its position in space is removed. Its *locality*, therefore, is *derivative* and contingently applied to it, *not primitive* and a necessary condition of its existence, because whatever things cannot by themselves be objects of external senses such as man's, that is, *immaterial* substances, are exempt altogether from the universal condition of *externally sensible things*, namely, space. Hence absolute and immediate locality may be denied to the soul, while yet hypothetical and mediate locality may be attributed to it.

PART III

DEVELOPMENTS OF THE DISSERTATION

COMPARATIVELY little need be added to set forth the relation of the *Dissertation* to the Critical System. We have designedly anticipated much in order to indicate from the first the point of view for contemplating the Dissertation as a turning-point in the development of the philosophy of Kant.

1. Comments of Lambert and Mendelssohn

Lambert, whose *Kosmologische Briefe* unintentionally reproduced Kant's opinion on the origin of the starry heavens half a dozen years after its appearance, agreed with Kant as to the methodical need in metaphysics of invention and renovation. The universality which is to prevail in it, he wrote, aims in a certain sense for omniscience, and to that extent beyond the limits of human cognition. It seems to me it has always been an unrecognized but chief mistake of philosophers to wish to force things. Rather than leave aught unexpounded, they have satisfied themselves with hypotheses, which in fact have delayed the discovery of truth.[1]

The agreement between him and Kant was even more definite. Kant for several years had turned his philosophical considerations in every conceivable direction, and after being upset many times, and each time seeking the sources of error or insight in the method of procedure, deemed him-

[1] VIII, 657.

self sure finally of the method to be observed in order to escape that mirage of knowledge which causes us to believe every moment that we have reached a decision, only to compel us as often to retrace our steps; whence originates also the ruinous dissension of those imagining themselves philosophers, there being no common standard to give consonancy to their efforts.[1] In giving this bit of autobiography, Kant plainly referred to the Inquiries into the Evidentness of the Principles of Natural Theology and Morals. Lambert replies: The method which you, sir, indicate in your letter, is beyond contradiction the only one that can be used safely and with good progress.[2] The attitude of both men towards the rationalistic philosophy was the question: Whether and to what extent the knowledge of the form of that which we know leads to the knowledge of the matter of that which we know, and both hit upon comparing philosophical with mathematical cognitions. The only effect of this correspondence shown in segregate form in the Critique is referred to by Kant in a letter to Bernouilli:[3] "The excellent man offered objections to the concepts of time and space. I answered them in the Critique of Pure Reason." The objection appears in a letter of Lambert's of December, 1770, the answer in the Elementarlehre I Theil, II Abschnitt, paragraph 7, under the appropriate heading of Erläuterung, being in fact a mere elucidation.

Mendelssohn's objection to Kant's averment: I do not understand the signification of the word *after*, unless by the antecedent conception of time,[4] that this difficulty seems to prove the poverty of language rather than an incorrectness of concepts, made even less impression of a separately indicable nature on Kant. That it was one of many influences

[1] VIII, 655.   [2] VIII, 657.
[3] VIII, 650.   [4] II, 406.

leading to the Kantian exclusion of empirical psychology from metaphysics[1] is very probable.

Mendelssohn's view of the evolutional relation of the *Dissertation* to the Critique is precisely that which we have suggested. Writing to Kant he says: Obviously this pamphlet is the fruit of long meditation, and must be regarded as a portion of a whole system of doctrine peculiar to the author, and of which for the present he is willing to show but few samples. The apparent obscurity itself which has remained in some places betrays to a practiced reader a relation to a whole not yet presented.[2]

2. *The Relation of the Dissertation to Transcendental Dialectic*

This relation to a whole is to be found in the Critique, the Dissertation passing almost certainly through the intermediate stage of a work under the title of The Boundaries of Sensuousness and Reason,[3] which was never published.

As the Dissertation was transferred almost in bulk, one has one's choice of two methods of treatment. One may be very elaborate or one may be very brief. The latter alternative, of necessity, we adopt.

The relative importance of parts of the Dissertation is stated by the author himself: The First and Fourth sections may be passed over as unimportant, but the Second, Third and Fifth, although owing to indisposition I have not gotten them up at all satisfactorily to myself, seem to me to contain a matter well worth a more careful and extensive elaboration. The most general propositions regarding sensibility play falsely a great rôle in metaphysics, though in the latter the only question is of concepts and principles of pure reason.[4]

[1] Methodenlehre, III, Hptst.   [2] VIII, 676.
[3] VIII, 686.   [4] VIII, 663.

That is to say, Kant emphasizes the principles of the form of the sensible world,[1] and their discrimination from noumena[2] in the method of metaphysics.[3] We accordingly find that, roughly speaking, Section III enters into the Critique as the Transcendental Aesthetics, while Sections II and V form the ground-stock of Transcendental Analytics, the unemphasized First and Fourth sections containing the scattered seeds of the Transcendental Dialectics.

The number of these germs is apt to be under-estimated. We shall intimate a few.

In the teeth of Mendelssohn's objection the implication of time in the Principle of Contradiction is retained in the definition of change and the accidental. In the pure sense of the Categories we call contingent that of which the contradictory opposite is possible. Of what undergoes change we may say that the opposite of its state is real—and therefore possible also—at another time.[4]

Kant continues to hold that we can discover no sign of contingency except something *happening*, that is, the existence preceded by the non-existence of the object.[5]

The proposition that the world must have a beginning in time, is still classified as a *transcendental illusion*.[6]

The remainder turns up again that there exist in our reason considered subjectively as a faculty of human knowledge principles and maxims of its use, which have the appearance of objective principles and lead us to mistake the subjective necessity of a certain connection of our concepts in favor of the understanding for an objective necessity inherent in the determination of things themselves.[7]

Occasionally we have a curious shifting in the terminology,

[1] Sectio III. [2] Sectio II. [3] Sectio V. [4] III, 326.
[5] III, 521. [6] III, 246. [7] Ibid.

especially in the Critical re-adjustment of the Intelligible World of the Dissertation. I call all transcendental ideas as to the absolute totality in the synthesis of phenomena *cosmical concepts*, partly because of the unconditioned totality upon which rests the concept of the cosmical universe—itself only an idea—partly, because they refer only to the synthesis of phenomena, which is empirical. The absolute totality in the synthesis of conditions must produce an ideal of pure reason. This ideal is totally different from the cosmical concept, though in a sense related to it.[1] Toward the end, we observe, the re-adjustment is barred. We find discussed, as in the Dissertation, since everything comprehended under phenomena is changeable, and, therefore, conditioned in its existence, an unconditioned member the existence of which may be considered as absolutely necessary . . . . a necessary being.[2] We are, of course, made to know its Critical transcendental place.

These Dialectic ideas, Kant persists in instructing us, are introduced in the interest of reason, that is, for the establishment of certain principles and to introduce systematical unity into our knowledge.[3] But the Transcendental ideal is still the archetype or Prototypon transcendentale.[4]

Phenomena and space are as emphatically as ever the matter and the form in one and the same empirical intuition.[5]

We are again enjoined never to dispense with the extension of the empirical use of the understanding,[6] that is, not to indulge lazy reason,[7] though empirical arguments cannot produce apodictic proof.[8]

He still holds, the idea is quite correct which sets up the maximum as an archetype,[9] negations being nothing but *limitations*, which they could not be unless there were the substratum of the unlimited, the All.[10]

[1] III, 293.   [2] III, 387.   [3] III, 439.   [4] III, 393.   [5] III, 307, note.
[6] III, 364.   [7] III, 462, 512.   [8] III, 490.   [9] III, 259.   [10] III, 396.

Still, once more, we must not on that ground cease to employ the subordinate faculty for imparting logical form to any given knowledge, the faculty by which the cognitions of the understanding are arranged among themselves only, lower rules under higher, the condition of the latter comprehending the condition of the former, as far as all this can be done through comparison.[1]

It is impossible to allow transcendental hypotheses in the speculative employment of reason, or the use of hyperphyssical instead of physical explanations; and again on the Dissertational ground, because reason is thus not in the least advanced.[2]

In the Critique not less than in the Dissertation, there would be no excuse if reason were to surrender a causality which it knows, and have recourse to obscure indemonstrable principles of explanation, which it does not know.[3]

We have two expressions, *world* and *nature*, which frequently run into each other. The first denotes the mathematical total of phenomena and the totality of their synthesis, either by composition or division. The world, however, is called nature if we look upon it as a dynamical whole, and consider not the aggregation of space and time, which produces quantity, but the unity in the existence of phenomena.[4]

It might be supposed that this is only an economical trick of the reason for the purpose of saving itself trouble, a purely hypothetical attempt which, if successful, would impart by that very unity a certain amount of probability to the presupposed principle of explanation. Such a selfish purpose, however, can easily be distinguished from the idea according to which we all presuppose that this unity of reason agrees with nature, and that in this case reason does not beg but bids, although we may be quite unable, as yet, to determine the limits of that unity.[5]

[1] III, 251. [2] III, 512. [3] III, 425. [4] III, 300. [5] III, 441.

As to the field of hypotheses, if the faculty of imagination is not simply to indulge in dreams, but to invent and compose under the strict surveillance of reason, it is necessary that there should always be something perfectly certain, and not only invented or resting on opinion, and that is the *possibility* of the object itself. If that is given, it is then allowable, so far as its reality is concerned, to have recourse to opinion.[1]

This opinion, however, if it is not to be utterly groundless, must be brought in connection with what is really given, and, therefore, certain as its ground of explanation.[2]

This principle of complete determination relates to the content and not only to the logical form.[3]

According to this principle, therefore, everything is referred to a common correlate, that is, to the total possibility which, could it, the matter for all possible predicates, be found in the idea of any single thing, would prove an affinity of all possible things, through the identity of the ground of complete determination.[4]

Here we reach again one of these re-adjustments of thought so interesting to observe in the development of the Critique from the Dissertation.

We take the idea of supreme wisdom for our rule in the investigation of nature, and for the principle of its systematical and well-planned unity according to general laws, even when we are not able to perceive that unity.[5]

In other words, it must be the same to you, wherever you perceive it, whether you say, God has wisely willed it so, or nature has wisely arranged it so.[6]

The *sophisma figurae dictionis* is shown up in the paralogism of rational psychology and in the Cosmological conflict.[7]

[1] III, 510.   [2] Ibid.   [3] III, 394.   [4] Ibid., note.
[5] III, 467.   [6] Ibid.   [7] III, 352.

Reason still follows its own course in its empirical, and again a peculiar course in its transcendental use,¹ and Kant keeps us in mind of the Dissertational origin of his idea of the transcendental use of reason by saying: Whatever in an object of the senses is not in itself phenomenal, I call *intelligible*.²

But a truce to quotations, the food of the bookworm.

3. *The Relation of the Dissertation to Transcendental Æsthetic and Analytic, illustrated from the Amphiboly of Reflective Concepts*

It would be impossible to pursue the plan of citation with the Transcendental Analytics, where the originative part of the Dissertation is so much greater. Compact excerpts of paragraphs and pages would be required to represent this influence adequately. Nay, coincidences in words and turns of phrase grow thick; even the alter hircum mulgere, alter cribrum supponere³ is there.⁴

The case is still stronger, of course, for the Transcendental Aesthetics. Strip it of its more careful and extensive elaborations, that is, get rid of the Erläuterung above referred to and its congeners, and you have the Dissertation.

Instead of trying to place upon our pages what they cannot hold, let us proceed to the end of the Transcendental Aesthetics and Analytics, to the border of the Transcendental Dialectics, whose less solid but still perceptible connection with the Dissertation has been illustrated. Kant's Anmerkung zur Amphibolie der Reflexionsbegriffe, by its cogent, logical and historical presentation, will not only set forth far better than any array of disjointed quotations the true import of the two parts of the Critique, which it con-

¹ III, 388.   ² III, 374.   ³ II, 420.
⁴ Dass Einer den Bock melkt, der Andere ein Sieb unterhält, III, 86.

cludes, but shed a flood of light on their relation to the Dissertation. We have appropriated from it already the plea for the term "transcendental place," when confessing our inability to be as certain as a writer whom we greatly respect in reference to the particular origin of the Dissertation. Kant says: For want of such a transcendental topic, and deceived by the amphiboly of reflective concepts, the celebrated Leibnitz erected an *intellectual system of the world*, or believed at least that he knew the internal nature of things by comparing all objects by the understanding only and by the abstract formal concepts of his mind. Comparing all things with each other by means of concepts only, he naturally found no other difference but those by which the understanding distinguishes its pure concepts from each other. The conditions of sensuous intuition, which carry their own differences, are not considered by him as original and independent; for sensibility was with him a confused mode of representation only, and not a separate source of representations. According to him, a phenomenon was the representation of the thing itself, though different, in its logical form, from knowledge by means of the understanding, because the phenomenon, in the ordinary absence of analysis, brings a certain admixture of collateral representations into the concept of a thing which the understanding is able to separate. In one word, Leibnitz *intellectualized* phenomena, just as Locke, according to his system of Noögony, if I may use such an expression, *sensualized* all concepts of the understanding, that is, represented them as nothing but empirical, although abstract, reflective concepts. Instead of regarding the understanding and sensibility as two totally distinct sources of representation, which however can supply objectively valid judgments of things only in conjunction with each other, each of these great men recognized but one of them. This one, in their opinion, applied immediately to things themselves, while the other did nothing but to produce either disorder or order in the representations of the former.

Leibnitz, accordingly, compared the objects of the senses with each other as things in general and in the understanding only. He did this, *first*, so far as they are judged by the understanding to be either identical or different. As he considers their concepts only and not their place in intuition, in which alone objects can be given, and takes no account of the transcendental place of these concepts—whether the object is to be counted among phenomena or among things themselves—it could not happen otherwise than that he should extend his principle of indiscernibility, which is valid with regard to concepts of things in general, to objects of the senses also (mundus phenomenon) and imagine that he thus extended not inconsiderably our knowledge of nature. No doubt, if I know a drop of water as a thing itself in all its internal determinations, I cannot allow that one is different from the other, when their entire concepts are identical.

Secondly, the principle that realities as mere assertions never logically contradict each other is perfectly true with regard to the relation of concepts, but has no meaning whatever, either as regards nature or as regards that of which we have no concept whatever, namely, a thing itself. Real opposition, as when A—B=o, takes place wherever two realities being united in one subject, one reality annihilates the effect of the other. This is constantly brought before us in nature by all impediments and reactions which, depending on forces, must be called *realitates phenomena*.

Thirdly, the Leibnitzian monadology has really no other foundation than that Leibnitz represented the difference of the internal and external in relation to the understanding only. Substances must have something *internal*, which is free from all external relations, and therefore from composition. The simple, therefore, the uncompounded, is the foundation of the internal, of things themselves. The internal in substances cannot consist in space, form, contact, or motion, all these determinations being external relations. We cannot, therefore, ascribe to substances any internal state but that which belongs to our own internal sense, namely, the *state of representations*. This is the history of the monads which were to form the elements of the whole universe, and the energy of which consists in representations only, so that properly only within themselves can they be active.

For this reason, the principle of a possible community of substances could only be a pre-established harmony, not a physical influence.

Fourthly, Leibnitz's celebrated doctrine of space and time, in which he intellectualized these forms of sensibility, arose entirely from the same delusion of transcendental reflection. If by the pure understanding alone I want to represent the external relations of things, I can do this only by means of the concept of their reciprocal action; if I want to connect one state with another state of the same thing, this is possible only in the order of cause and effect. Thus it happened that Leibnitz conceived space as a certain order in the community of substances, and time as the dynamical sequence of their states.

That which space and time seem to possess as proper to themselves and independent of things, he ascribed to the confusion of these concepts, which made us mistake what is a mere form of dynamical relations for a peculiar and independent intuition, antecedent to things themselves. Thus space and time became with him the intelligible form of the connection of things themselves, namely of substances and their states, all things being intelligible substances (substantiæ noumena). Nevertheless, he tried to make these concepts equal to phenomena, because he would not concede to sensibility any independent kind of intuition, but ascribed all, even the empirical representation of objects, to the understanding, leaving to the senses nothing but the contemptible work of confusing and mutilating the representations of the understanding.

What renders this criticism of conclusions by acts of mere reflection extremely useful is, that it shows clearly the nullity of all conclusions with regard to objects compared with each other in the understanding only, and that it confirms at the same time what we have so strongly insisted on, namely, that phenomena, though they cannot be comprehended as things themselves among the objects of the pure understanding, are, nevertheless, the only objects in which our knowledge can possess objective reality, i. e., where intuition corresponds to concepts.

If this Kantian account of the difference between Criticism and Leibnitzianism is not, within the limits we have assigned, applicable to the Dissertation, we are mistaken.

4. *Conclusion—A Question and an Answer*

If the *Dissertation* be all that we have argued it to be, how is it that its publication was followed by what may be called the *silent decade?*

Because after the turning-point, a number of other points had to be reached, some of them far apart.

But how did it come to take so long, and what influences were at work?

That is an interesting question, requiring a separate chapter. But before it can be written, one point must be definitely settled.

After all, are we right in taking the Dissertation for the turning-point?

If we are not, then the turning-point falls somewhere

within the silent decade. If we are, then Kant, having entered the right road, plodded silently on in the direction indicated by the Dissertation as a guide-post till he reached the goal, the Critique of Pure Reason. In other words, if we are right, the Dissertation is the beginning of the end, though the end be afar off. It is the beginning of the Critical period. If we are not, it is the Pre-Critical. The Critical period begins somewhere else, and that somewhere else is later on.

We have been obliged to withhold assent from a very respectable position on the Dissertation. We are on the present occasion constrained, reluctantly, for a man of Professor Windelband's soberness and solidity of judgment is not rashly to be differed with, to cite Dr. Windelband adversatively to Kant and leave the matter to the decision of the reader.

According to Windelband, the system set forth in the *Dissertation* was promptly given up again, and, therefore, belongs to the Pre-Critical period. The doctrine presented with an appeal to Malebranche in Section IV is precisely the system of preformed harmony between cognition and reality which Kant so energetically rejects in his letter of the 21st of February, 1772, to Marcus Herz.[1]

The appeal to Malebranche does not seem to us very vigorous.[2] It is semi-deprecatory and wears the appearance rather of an obiter dictum than of an argument which the writer intends to take his stand on. It is unnecessary to insist on the fact that the passage in the letter to Herz refers to Crusius and not, as Windelband intimates, to Malebranche, the latter and Plato being distinctly classified otherwise, because Kant rejects the hyperphysical influence of Plato and Malebranche as much as the pre-established intellectual harmony of Crusius. It suffices to affirm that the only notice-

[1] Windelband, *Geschichte der Philosophie*, S. 383.
[2] See the Scholium to paragraph 22.

able difference between the Scholium and the passage in the letter is, that the former begins: If it were right to overstep the limits of certainty befitting metaphysics; while the latter concludes practically: But it isn't. Let the reader judge for himself. Here is the passage in full.

Plato assumed as the primal source of the pure concepts and principles of the understanding a former spiritual intuition of the deity, Malebranche a perennial intuition of this primal essence (or being, Urwesen) continuing even now. Several moralists have assumed the same in regard to the primary moral laws. Crusius assumes certain implanted rules of judgment and concepts implanted by God readymade, such as they must be in order to harmonize with objects. The former system might be called *influxus hyperphysicus*, the last one *harmonia praestabilita intellectualis*. But the *deus ex machina* in determining the origin and validity of our cognition is as completely without rhyme and reason as any choice one can make. Besides the deceptive circle in the conclusion concerning our cognition, it has the disadvantage of giving aid to the cobwebs of brains pious or subtilely fanciful.[1]

It is quite an intellectual habit with Kant, we wish to observe, to elaborate somebody's metaphysical view in Kantian phraseology in order to reject it. In the Critique the rejection is always accomplished with becoming ponderosity and hence is unmistakable. In earlier writings the elaboration is as full, but the rejection is sometimes only indicated. There is an historical instance parallel to what we cannot but consider Windelband's mistake.

In the *Dreams of a Ghost-Seer Elucidated by Dreams of Metaphysics*, Kant spoke as follows: It would be beautiful if such a systematic constitution of the spiritual world could be concluded, or at all events could be surmised with probabil-

[1] VIII, 690.

ity not merely from the general concept of the nature of a spirit, which is all too hypothetical, but from some actual and universally conceded observation. Presuming upon the reader's indulgence, I insert an attempt of the kind, somewhat out of my way, to be sure, and far from a demonstration, but nevertheless giving occasion, it seems to me, for not unpleasant surmises.

This intercalation[1] is very much in the nature of a Scholium, would gladden the heart of a Swedenborgian as much as this scholium would that of a follower of a Malebranche, ends in as retractive a manner as the scholium, and to complete the analogy, was mistaken by Mendelssohn as, we think, the scholium is by Windelband. Kant's reply to the former will answer the latter as well: "My attempt at an analogy is not really a serious opinion of mine, but an example how far one may unhindered go in philosophical fictions where we have no data, and how needful it is to determine what is necessary to the solution of the problem and whether the necessary data do not fail us;"[2] advice in substantial agreement, by the way, with the last sentence of the scholium itself.

Really, Windelband's—as the instance of Mendelssohn shows, far from unnatural—misunderstanding of an incidental exhibition of a Kantian peculiarity would not require to be mentioned if it were not part of that meritorious author's argument for relegating the Dissertation to the Pre-Critical period of Kant.

On this point, the following passage in a letter from Kant to his editor, Tieftrunk,[3] seems to us to put Windelband at issue with Kant himself: "I assent with pleasure to your proposal for collecting and editing my minor writings. Only I wish you would not include writings older than 1770. In this case, a German translation of my Inaugural *Dissertation*

[1] II, 342–345.   [2] VIII, 675.   [3] VIII, 812.

De Mundi Sensibilis et Intelligibilis might form the beginning." We cannot conceive why Kant should have drawn this line, unless he agreed with Mendelssohn and the present writer.

One's difficulty in thus conceiving is not fanciful, but implied in Kant's repugnance to having "writings no longer consonant with his present mode of thinking (*Denkart*)"[1] resurrected. The existence of the sentiment is none the less but rather the stronger argument for being not confined to Kant but a common one among men of intellectual self-respect. Feeling as Kant did, would he have drawn the line as he did, if Windelband were right?

[1] VIII, 596.

Augsburg College
George Sverdrup Library
Minneapolis, Minnesota 55404